Practical
Merchandising Math

National Retail Federation Series

The National Retail Federation Series comprises books on retail store management for stores of all sizes and for all management responsibilities. The National Retail Federation is the world's largest retail trade association, with membership that includes the leading department, specialty, discount, mass merchandise, and independent stores, as well as 30 national and 50 state associations. NRF members represent an industry that encompasses more than 1.4 million U.S. retail establishments and employs nearly 20 million people—1 in 5 American workers. The NRF's international members operate stores in more than 50 nations.

The National Retail Federation Series includes the following books.

Published Books:

Competing With the Retail Giants: How to Survive in the New Retail Landscape, by Kenneth E. Stone

Credit Card Marketing, by Bill Grady

Dictionary of Retailing and Merchandising, by Jerry M. Rosenberg

FOR 1995: Financial & Operating Results of Retail Stores in 1994, by the National Retail Federation

Loss Prevention Guide for Retail Businesses, by Rudolf C. Kimiecik

Management of Retail Buying, Third Edition, by R. Patrick Cash, John W. Wingate, and Joseph S. Friedlander

MOR 1995: Merchandising & Operating Results of Retail Stores in 1994, by the National Retail Federation

Retail Store Planning & Design Manual, Second Edition, by Michael Lopez

The Software Directory for Retailers, Fifth Edition, by Coopers & Lybrand

The Electronic Retailing Market: TV Home Shopping, Infomercials, and Interactive Retailing, by Packaged Facts, Inc.

Value Retailing in the 1990s: Off-Pricers, Factory Outlets, and Closeout Stores, by Packaged Facts, Inc.

Practical Merchandising Math, by Leo Gafney

Forthcoming Books:

Retail Marketing & Advertising: A Retailer's Guide to Maximizing Store Traffic & Sales, by Donald Ziccardi with David Moin

Specialty Shop Retailing: A Guide to Starting Your Own Shop, by Carol Schroeder

Practical Merchandising Math

Leo Gafney

John Wiley & Sons, Inc.

New York • Chichester • Brisbane • Toronto • Singapore

Library of Congress Cataloging-in-Publication Data:

Gafney, Leo.
    Practical merchandising math / Leo Gafney.
        p.   cm. — (National Retail Federation series)
    Includes bibliographical references.
    ISBN 0-471-14518-1 (paper)
    1. Business mathematics—Retail trade.   2. Merchandising.
    I. Title. II. Series.
    HF5695.5.R45G33 1996
    658.8′001′513—dc20   95-37072
                                                          CIP

Printed in the United States of America

10 9 8 7 6 5 4 3 2 1

Contents

Introduction

There are many aspects to retail business: prices, store location, discounts, employees, product selection, and bills to pay. The owner of a store or manager of a retail business can be overwhelmed in a sea of details. That is why it helps to maintain clarity about a few basic ideas.

This book is about the mathematics used in a retail business. The book will not help you decide what kind of a store to open, nor will it tell you about the most popular colors in shirts and dresses. But it will help you with all of the financial arrangements important to a retail business.

Business is fundamentally the art of buying and selling. Buy 100 shirts for $10 each and sell them for $15 each. You earn $5 for each shirt, or $500 for all 100 shirts. It's that simple. Or is it? If you don't own your store, you must pay rent. You have heating or air conditioning bills. You have employees to pay. You must earn enough to pay yourself. Maybe selling the shirts for $15 will not earn you enough money to cover business expenses.

So we must also include expenses as an important part of any business. Finally, to hold everything together, the retailer must keep records. He or she must know how much money the business needs, how much has been spent, and how much will be spent.

These four areas: buying, expenses, selling, and record keeping, form the four parts of this text. As you work through the details of topics such as markon, discount, inventory, and financial statements, you should keep in mind that they all relate to the four key ideas.

Finally, although each of the four ideas is the topic of a separate part, they cannot be considered apart from one another. As a retailer buys merchandise, she is thinking of selling. When a retailer records expenses, he begins to think about future purchases. And careful record keeping allows the retailer to see how the business has been going, and how it is likely to go in the future. So each of the four ideas is connected in many ways to the other three.

So maintain a businesslike attitude and keep your mind on the four big ideas: buying, expenses, selling, and record keeping.

Part I Purchasing and Pricing

1 Transportation Terms and Charges

Jodi Ortega owns a sweater store. She is always buying and selling sweaters. Her taste is excellent; whatever she buys, she sells. You might think her business is great. But there is one problem: delivery. If an order is on time, it is incomplete. If the order is complete, the goods are damaged. If the goods are in good condition, they are late. If everything seems to be okay, the delivery charges are too high. In other words, transportation is no simple matter. It may surprise you to find that there are many different ways to calculate the costs and responsibilities for transporting goods.

After completing this chapter you will be able to:

- Identify and explain different transportation terms.

- Determine who has title to goods during transportation.

- Use mathematical procedures to calculate the cost of transportation based on given transportation terms.

- Determine the effect of transportation terms on a retailer's cost price.

- Recognize a retailer's liabilities under different transportation terms.

It is important that goods be delivered at a time that will satisfy the customers' needs. Merchandise received too early may lose its appeal before the customers need it. Merchandise received too late will surely not satisfy customers' needs; people do not want to buy winter jackets in May. It is difficult to determine, however, exactly when each season begins and ends. It used to be that stores did not decorate for the Christmas holidays until after Thanksgiving. Now it seems that the holiday shopping season begins after Halloween. Indeed, there are stores that do a healthy business selling Christmas ornaments all year long.

TRANSPORTATION TERMS

Retailers naturally prefer the supplier to pay transportation charges. They also prefer that the supplier maintains title to the goods during transportation because whoever has title retains responsibility and will have to file and perhaps negotiate claims with insurance companies in cases of loss, damage, or theft. But there are many other factors involved in purchasing, and so the allocation of transportation costs is usually subject to negotiation.

The following vocabulary will be used in discussing transportation terms.

Claim: Request to an insurance company from an insured person for compensation caused by loss or damage to goods or property.

Cost Price: Actual cost of merchandise to the retailer.

Drop Ship: When the buyer orders merchandise shipped directly to a specific branch store, it is noted on the buyer's order: "Drop Ship to _____ ."

F.O.B.:   Free-On-Board, followed by a point of destination, indicates the place at which the title passes to the retailer.

Supplier, Vendor: The one selling goods to the buyer or retailer.

Title: Ownership. The time at which title passes from the seller to the buyer is important because certain costs and claims depend on ownership.

Transportation Terms: Arrangements that specify when title to goods passes to the retailer and whether the supplier or the retailer will pay for transportation charges.

Free-On-Board (F.O.B.) is always followed by a destination which determines:

A. When Title Passes, for example:

   1. *F.O.B. Store* means that title to the goods passes to the retailer when the merchandise reaches the store.

   2. *F.O.B. Factory* means that title to the goods passes to the retailer at the manufacturer's factory. The retailer assumes all liabilities from the factory to the store.

B. Who Pays the Transportation Charge, for example:

   1. *F.O.B. Store* means that the supplier pays all transportation charges.

   2. *F.O.B. Factory* means that the retailer pays all transportation charges from the factory to the store.

The following are some of the more commonly used transportation terms. They are ordered from most to least beneficial to the retailer. In each case, the first part of the term indicates when title passes from the supplier to the retailer. If there is no qualification in the term, this then also tells who pays the transportation charges. If there is a qualification, this then must be interpreted to determine how the transportation charges are to be paid.

   1. Supplier retains title during transportation. Full transportation costs are paid by the seller:
      F.O.B. Store
      F.O.B. Door
      F.O.B. Warehouse
      F.O.B. Distribution Center
      F.O.B. Destination

   2. The supplier retains title during transportation. The retailer pays transportation charges but deducts the charges when paying the supplier's invoice:
      F.O.B. Store, Freight Collect and Allowed

   3. The title passes to the retailer at the point of origin, but the supplier pays transportation.
      F.O.B. Factory, Freight Prepaid

4. The supplier retains title during transportation, but the retailer pays transportation charges:

F.O.B. Store, Charges Reversed

5. The retailer takes title to the goods and pays transportation from the point of origin:

F.O.B. Origin

F.O.B. Factory

Table 1–1 summarizes the meanings of the different terms.

Example 1:

Alan Benedict & Sons, Inc., a retail clothing chain, purchases 2,000 shirts from the Allday Shirt Co. Terms are: F.O.B. Warehouse, Freight Collect and Allowed.

a. Who holds title during transportation?

b. Who pays the transportation charges?

c. Is any further action required regarding the transportation charges?

Solution:

a. F.O.B. Warehouse means that the supplier, Allday Shirt Co., holds title.

TABLE 1–1

Transportation Terms

Terms	Title	Transportation Charges
F.O.B. Store, Door, or Destination	Supplier retains title during transportation	Supplier pays transportation charges
F.O.B. Store, Freight Collect and Allowed	Supplier retains title during transportation	Retailer pays transportation charges and deducts them from the invoice
F.O.B. Store, Charges Reversed	Supplier retains title during transportation	Retailer pays transportation charges
F.O.B. Origin	Retailer takes title at point of origin	Retailer pays transportation charges

b. Freight Collect means that the retailer, Alan Benedict & Sons, pays the transportation charges.

c. The transportation charges are subtracted from the invoice amount when Alan Benedict & Sons pays Allday Shirt Co.

Example 2:

A retailer, located in Los Angeles, makes a purchase from a supplier in Dallas, with terms F.O.B. Dallas.

a. When does the retailer take title to the goods?

b. Does the retailer pay any transportation charges? If so, from what point to what point?

Solution:

a. The retailer takes title to the goods at the point listed after F.O.B., that is, Dallas.

b. The retailer pays the transportation charges from Dallas to the store in Los Angeles.

PRACTICE

For Problems 1–6, determine: (a) who holds title during transportation; (b) who pays the transportation charges and whether any further action is required regarding the transportation charges.

1. Hi–Y, a food store, purchases milk from the ABX Dairy. Terms are F.O.B. Store.

2. Jason Danton, a buyer for Peabody Clothiers, purchases clothing from Cotton Goods, Inc. Terms are F.O.B. Store, Charges Reversed.

3. Melissa Crafts sells earrings and necklaces to Jewelry Town. Terms are F.O.B. Origin.

4. Sports City purchases equipment from Run Around, Inc. Terms are F.O.B. Warehouse, Freight Collect and Allowed.

5. Footwear, Inc., sells goods to Jean & Gene. Terms are F.O.B. Store, Charges Reversed.

6. A retailer in Newark, New Jersey, purchases goods from a supplier in Tulsa, Oklahoma. The terms are F.O.B. Tulsa.

Complete Table 1–2, indicating when title passes from the supplier to the retailer and who pays transportation charges.

TABLE 1–2

Determining Title and Transportation Charges

Terms	Title	Transportation Charges
F.O.B. Store	7. _____	8. _____
F.O.B. Store, Freight Collect and Allowed	9. _____	10. _____
F.O.B. Factory, Freight Prepaid	11. _____	12. _____
F.O.B. Store, Charges Reversed	13. _____	14. _____
F.O.B. Origin	15. _____	16. _____

ANSWERS

1. (a) ABX Dairy, the supplier, holds title during transit, (b) ABX pays for transportation.

2. (a) Cotton Goods, the supplier, holds title during transit, (b) Peabody pays transportation.

3. (a) Jewelry Town, the retailer, holds title, (b) Jewelry Town pays transportation.

4. (a) Run Around, Inc., the supplier, holds title, (b) Sports City, the retailer, pays the transportation charges and then deducts them from the invoice.

5. (a) Footwear, Inc., the supplier, holds title, (b) Jean & Gene, the retailer, pays transportation charges.

6. (a) The retailer takes title in Tulsa, (b) the retailer pays transportation charges.

7. Supplier holds title during transit.

8. Supplier pays transportation charges.

9. Supplier holds title during transit.

10. Retailer pays transportation charges and deducts them from the invoice.

11. Retailer takes title during transit.

12. Supplier pays transportation charges.

13. Supplier holds title during transit.

14. Retailer pays transportation charges.

15. Retailer holds title during transit.

16. Retailer pays transportation charges.

<u>   2</u>   Terms and Dating

In addition to transportation terms, which deal with transfer of title and transportation charges, goods sold from a supplier to a retailer are also affected by dating terms. These terms specify how the amount to be paid depends on the time when payment is made.

After completing this chapter you will be able to:

- Explain the meaning of given dating terms.

- Use discount percents to calculate costs after discount.

- Determine the amount to be paid based on dating terms.

■ MATH REVIEW: FINDING THE PERCENT OF A NUMBER

Percent means parts out of 100. Any percent can be converted to a decimal by moving the decimal point two places to the left. When there is no decimal point shown, the decimal is understood to be at the end of the number. For example, 25% can be written as 0.25.

To find the percent of a number, convert the percent to a decimal and then multiply by the number.

For example, to find 25% of $45, first convert 25% to a decimal, then multiply the decimal by $45.

$$25\% = 0.25$$
$$0.25 \times 45 = 11.25$$

Therefore, 25% of $45 equals $11.25.

Discount is an amount deducted from a cost or selling price. The amount to be deducted is based on percent.

For example, the invoice for a shipment shows a cost price of $786.50 with a 2% discount for payment under certain terms. To determine the price after the discount find first the amount of the discount, then subtract the discount amount to determine the amount to be paid.

1. Discount Amount: $786.50 \times 0.02 = 15.73$.

2. Invoice Payment: $786.50 - 15.73 = \$770.77$.

2.1 TERMS

Retail businesses do not usually pay suppliers' invoices as soon as merchandise is received. A retailer may have many bills to pay at one time and he or she will, therefore, pay some and delay paying others. Suppliers prefer to be paid as quickly as possible. In order to encourage retailers to pay more quickly, suppliers often offer discounts for payment within a certain number of days. This discount for payment in a given time period is called a *cash discount.*

In addition to the cash discount, suppliers generally also specify the time in which full payment is expected. After that time, the retailer may have to pay a finance charge in addition to the amount stated on the invoice.

A typical statement of ordinary discount terms is:

2/10/N30

Each number and letter has a meaning:

2: A discount of 2% is offered.

10: The discount may be taken if payment is made within 10 days.

N: This stands for the net, which is the actual amount of the invoice including any other discounts or fees.

30: The net amount must be paid within 30 days.

Dates are calculated from the date of the invoice.

Example 1:

A buyer makes a purchase of hardware on March 15 with terms of 2/10/N30.

   a. What is the percent of the cash discount if the invoice is paid on time?

   b. How many days does the supplier allow for payment of the invoice with a cash discount?

   c. What is the last date for payment of this invoice with a cash discount allowance?

   d. How many days does the supplier allow for payment of the invoice without a cash discount?

   e. What is the last date for payment of this invoice without a cash discount?

Solution:

   a. Since the first number is 2, a 2% discount is allowed.

   b. The second number is 10. Therefore, the supplier is allowing the retailer 10 days for payment of the invoice with a discount allowance.

   c. To find the last date for the discount allowance:

Write the date of the invoice	March 15
Write the number of days allowed for discount	+ 10
Add the days allowed to the date	25

The last date for the discount is March 25.

d. N30 means that the supplier allows 30 days for payment.

e. To find the last day for payment:

Write the date of the invoice	March 15
Write the number of days allowed for discount	+ 30
Add the days allowed to the date	45
March does not have 45 days. Therefore, subtract the number of days in March	− 31
The last day for payment is April 14	14

VARIABLE TERMS

To encourage early payment for goods, suppliers sometimes offer a sliding scale of discounts. For example, with the discount terms 5/30/4/60, a discount of 5% may be deducted if payment is made within 30 days and a discount of 4% may be deducted if payment is made between 30 and 60 days from the date of the invoice.

Example:

A retailer receives a shipment of goods purchased. The invoice date is September 21. The terms are 5/30/4/60.

a. Find the last date for which the 5% discount is allowed.

b. Find the last date for which the 4% discount is allowed.

Solution:

a. To find the last date for the 5% discount allowance:

Write the date of the invoice	September 21
Write the number of days allowed for discount	+ 30
Add the days allowed to the date	51
September does not have 51 days. Therefore, subtract the number of days in September	− 30
The last day for payment is October 21	21

b. To find the last date for the 4% discount allowance:

Write the date of the invoice	September 21
Write the number of days allowed for discount	+ 60
Add the days allowed to the date	81
September does not have 81 days. Therefore, subtract the number of days in September	− 30
	51
October does not have 51 days. Therefore, subtract the number of days in October	− 31
The last day for payment is November 20	20

PRACTICE 2.1

The following terms are stated on a supplier's invoice: 3/20/N30.

1. What is the percent cash discount offered?

2. For how many days is the cash discount offered?

3. What is the meaning of N30?

A buyer makes a purchase on June 21 with terms of 2/10/N30.

4. How many days does the supplier allow for payment of the invoice with a cash discount?

5. What is the last date for payment of this invoice with a cash discount allowance?

6. How many days does the supplier allow for payment of the invoice?

7. What is the last date for payment of this invoice without a cash discount?

The following terms are indicated on a supplier's invoice: 4/30/3/40. The invoice is dated April 11. Find each of the following.

8. The percent of cash discount if the invoice is paid within 30 days.

9. The percent of cash discount if the invoice is paid within 40 days.

10. The last day for payment that will allow the first discount.

11. The last day for payment that will allow the second discount.

An invoice contains the terms 3/30/2/45. It is dated June 20.

12. What percent discount is allowed if the invoice is paid on June 30?

13. What percent discount is allowed if payment is made on August 2?

14. What percent discount is allowed if payment is made on July 30?

An invoice dated August 28 lists terms: 5/30/4/60/3/90. Find:

15. The last date for a payment with a 5% cash discount.

16. The last date for a payment with a 4% cash discount.

17. The last date for a payment with a 3% cash discount.

2.2   CALCULATING THE DISCOUNT AND INVOICE PAYMENT AMOUNTS

You have learned to use cash discount terms to calculate the time frame and particular dates for which certain discounts are allowed. We now turn to the calculation of the discount amount for particular purchases and terms.

If your calculator has a percent key, you may then be able to calculate discounts and other percentages quickly using this key. For example, to find 2% of $245 with certain calculators you must enter the following key strokes: 245 × 2%. The display or printout will then show 4.90. But not all calculators work this way.

In this text we will determine discount amounts and other percentages by converting the percent to a decimal and then multiplying.

Example:

An invoice for $587 is dated January 17 and contains the cash discount terms 2/10/N30.

a. Find the last date for which the cash discount is allowed.

b. Find the amount of the discount.

c. Find the amount of the invoice to be paid after the discount is taken.

Solution:

a. Ten days from January 17 is January 27. This is the last day of the discount period.

b. The amount of the discount is found using the following steps:

1. Convert 2% to a decimal: 2% = 0.02.

2. Multiply the invoice amount by the percent: 587 × 0.02 = 11.74.

3. Subtract the discount: $587.00 − $11.74 = $575.26.

PRACTICE 2.2

Bigtown Sand & Gravel Co. sells and delivers cinder blocks, sand, and cement to Cushman Building Supplies. The invoice accompanying the delivery is dated February 18. The year is not a leap year. The amount of the invoice is $3,024. The cash discount terms are 5/30/4/60.

1. Find the last date for which a 5% discount is allowed.

2. What percent discount is allowed if the invoice is paid on March 19?

3. What is the dollar amount of the discount if the invoice is paid on April 2?

4. What amount must be paid on April 2?

Alice's Book Store purchases books from R. G. Xavier Publishing Co. The amount of the invoice is $912. The invoice is dated March 5. The transportation terms are F.O.B. Store. The cash discount terms are 2/20/N/60.

5. Who pays for the transportation of the books to the store?

6. When does Alice take title to the books?

7. If Alice pays the invoice on March 21, what is the dollar amount of discount?

8. What invoice amount must Alice pay on March 21?

9. If Alice pays on April 20, how much must she pay?

10. What is the last day for payment of the net amount?

2.3 END-OF-MONTH TERMS AND DATING

In some areas of the clothing industry it was once common for buyers to visit their suppliers several days a week. The terms 2/10/N30 were in effect. As a result, invoices had to be paid almost every day in order to take advantage of the discount.

Both retailer and supplier realized that these arrangements caused bookkeeping and accounting problems. It was then agreed that the term *End-of-Month* (E.O.M.) would be useful. This method would allow a buyer to make frequent visits to a supplier, but the retailer would only have to make one payment per month.

With the cash discount terms 8/10 E.O.M., an 8% discount is allowed for 10 days from the end of the month. This will always be the 10th of the following month.

RECEIPT-OF-GOODS TERMS AND DATING

Suppliers complete and date invoices at the time goods are shipped. Merchandise shipped a long distance may arrive during, or even toward the close of, the discount period. For example, a shipment across the country might begin on a freight train and then be transferred to trucks. The whole trip might take six or eight days of a ten-day discount period.

Retailers did not wish to lose the benefit of all or part of the time of discount, and so the term *Receipt-of-Goods* (R.O.G.) was introduced.

Receipt-of-Goods means that calculation of the days for discount and net payment begin on the day when the goods are received by the retailer.

With the terms 8/10 R.O.G., a discount of 8% is allowed for 10 days from the date on which the goods are received.

Example 1:

A purchase of $792 is made on November 13 with the terms 8/10 E.O.M.

    a. What percent discount is allowed?

    b. What is the last date on which the discount is allowed?

    c. What is the amount of payment after the discount?

Solution:

    a. The terms' first number is 8. Therefore, 8% is the discount.

    b. Ten days after the end of November is December 10.

    c. Discount: $792 \times 0.08 = \$63.36$; amount of payment: $792 - $63.36 = \$728.64$.

Example 2:

A shipment of goods has terms 2/10/N30 R.O.G. The purchase is made on March 20, but the goods are received on April 9. Find:

    a. The last date to make payment to obtain the cash discount.

    b. The last date to make payment without the cash discount.

Solution:

    a. The discount is allowed until 10 days from receipt of goods. The goods are received. That date is April 9.

    b. The invoice must be paid within 30 days from receipt of goods, that is, until May 9.

PRACTICE 2.3

A purchase of $1,476 has an invoice date of September 24 with terms 10/10 E.O.M.

1. What is the last date that the discount is allowed?

2. What is the dollar amount of the discount?

3. What is the amount of payment if the invoice is paid on October 8?

A shipment of furniture has terms 2/10/N30 R.O.G. The purchase is made on May 5, but the goods are received on June 10. The supplier is Oakridge Furniture Co. The retailer is Home Beauty Store. The amount of the invoice is $2,351.

4. Find the last date to make payment to obtain the cash discount.

5. Find the last date to make payment without the cash discount.

6. Who is buying the furniture?

7. What is the discount percent if the bill is paid on June 20?

8. How much must be paid if the bill is paid on June 20?

Goods are shipped from the ABX Company to Hanover Store with transportation terms: F.O.B. Factory, Freight Prepaid.

9. Who has title to the goods while in transit?

10. Who pays the transportation charges?

The accountant for a retail store looks at an invoice for $978 dated July 16 and reads the following terms: 5/15/4/30/N/60.

11. What is the dollar discount if the invoice is paid on August 1?

12. What payment is required if the invoice is paid on August 1?

13. What amount must be paid on September 15?

14. What amount must be paid on July 20?

The Athlete's World purchases an order of athletic shoes from The Running Co. The cash discount terms are 2/10/N30 R.O.G. The transportation terms are F.O.B. Store, Freight Collect and Allowed. The amount of the invoice is $630. The transportation charges are $42.50. The invoice is dated October 20. The shipment arrives at The Athlete's World on November 15.

15. Some of the merchandise is damaged in transit. Who files the claims with the insurance company?

16. How are the transportation charges paid?

17. If the invoice is paid on December 9, what amount must be paid?

18. If the invoice is paid on November 21, what is the percent discount?

19. If the invoice is paid on November 21, what is the dollar discount?

20. What is the amount of invoice payment on November 21?

2.4   ADVANCE, POST, SEASONAL, AND "AS OF" TERMS AND DATING

It sometimes happens that a manufacturer or vendor wants to ship goods in advance of a retailer's needs. The supplier may want to make room in the warehouse or may want the retailer's commitment to purchase. In the case of advance shipment, the supplier knows that it would interfere with the retailer's business to ask for payment long in advance of potential sales.

The solution to the problem is that the vendor and retailer will agree to early shipment but payment will be delayed. *Advance* refers to the shipment that is advanced, or moved forward, so that the goods arrive before they are needed. *Post* means "after" and refers to the dating of the invoice, which is after the delivery of goods. For example, the terms

2/10/E.O.M. or 8/10 E.O.M. might be accompanied by an invoice dated October 1, even though shipment of goods is made on September 1.

Seasonal dating refers to the fact that many consumer items, particularly clothes, change with the seasons. Suppliers will try to induce buyers to plan and order ahead to have their merchandise ready in advance of the next season. One of the incentives to do this is the practice of postdating.

In practice, "advanced," "post," and "seasonal" all refer to the same method.

As of dating is similar to the methods described above except that the date is sometimes determined months in advance when the shipping date is not known. For example, a buyer of toys might place orders in February to insure delivery in October. Since the manufacturer cannot pinpoint the delivery date so far in advance, the supplier and the retailer will agree upon a certain date when computation of the terms will take effect.

Orders for toys placed on February 15 might receive terms and dating of 2/10/N30 as of October 15. Payment computation will begin with the October 15th date regardless of the purchase date or the delivery date of the shipment. The date following the words "as of" is the date used to make cash discount computations.

Example:

A purchase of fur-lined coats is made on July 1. The order is received on September 1 with an invoice for $4,500. The invoice is dated October 1. The terms are 2/10/N30.

    a. Find the discount percent and the last date of payment with discount allowed.

    b. Find the amount of payment if the invoice is paid on October 8.

Solution:

    a. 2/10 means that a 2% discount is offered until 10 days after the invoice date, that is, until October 11.

    b. Discount: $4{,}500 \times 0.02 = 90$; payment: $4{,}500 - 90 = 4{,}410$; $4,410 is to be paid.

PRACTICE 2.4

A shipment of bathing suits is received on March 1, but is dated April 1 The terms are 2/10/N30. The invoice is for $1,340.

1. What is the last day for payment with the discount allowed?

2. What is the dollar amount of the discount if the invoice is paid in the allotted time?

3. What is the amount of payment if the invoice is paid on April 15?

A buyer purchases merchandise on March 1. She plans to accept shipment of the goods June 1. The supplier offers to date the invoice June 15 if the buyer will accept the shipment on May 1. The terms are 3/10/N30. The invoice amount is $561.

4. Find the last date to make payment and to obtain the cash discount.

5. Find the last date to make payment without the cash discount.

6. Find the invoice amount if payment is made on June 20.

A supplier offers terms of 8/10 E.O.M. and an invoice dated December 1 if the retailer accepts delivery on November 1. The invoice is for $1,020.

7. Find the last date to make payment and to obtain the discount.

8. Find the dollar amount of the discount offered.

A buyer for a toy store makes a purchase on April 20. The cash discount terms are 3/10/N30 as of October 15. The amount of the invoice is $786.

9. If delivery is on October 5, determine the last day for which the discount is allowed.

10. Find the amount to be paid if payment is made on October 20.

A purchase of $598 is made on March 1. The merchandise is received on September 1 with terms of 2/10/N30 as of September 15. The transportation terms are F.O.B. Factory.

11. Who has title while the goods are being transported?

12. Who pays the transportation charges?

13. What is the discount percent allowable?

14. What is the dollar discount if the invoice is paid on September 20?

15. What amount should be paid on September 20?

A purchase for $2,340 is made on January 20 with terms 8/10/ E.O.M. as of October 10. Delivery is made on October 1. Transportation terms are F.O.B. Store, Charges Reversed.

16. Find the last day for which the cash discount is allowed.

17. Find the dollar amount of the discount.

18. Find the amount if payment is made on October 15.

19. Who has title to the goods during transit?

20. Who pays transportation charges?

2.5   "EXTRA" TERMS AND DATING

Retailers, from time to time, experience problems that affect their ability to pay bills. Such problems include: costly expansion or remodeling of a store; losses caused by fire, flood, or vandalism; an economic slump that results in a delay in payment by the store's creditors.

As a result of the above or similar circumstances, a retailer may find it difficult to meet payment dates and consequently will ask for "extra" time for payment without loss of discount. By mutual agreement, the retailer and vendor may then use terms that include additional days during which the cash discount is allowed.

If the supplier's terms are 2/10/N30 and the agreement is for an extension of 60 extra days, the term is changed, so that it reads: 2/10–60X. The retailer is granted the regular 10 days plus 60 days extra, that is, a total of 70 days during which the 2% discount is allowed. The "N30" is removed since the retailer is expected to pay the full amount on or before the 70th day. The letter "X" stands for "extra."

Example:

A vendor's terms are 2/10/N30. The buyer requests 60 extra days because store renovations have tied up the retailer's funds. The supplier agrees to grant the extra 60 days and changes the terms to 2/10–60X. The invoice is dated June 10.

1. Find the last date for payment with the cash discount allowed.

2. Find the last date for payment without the cash discount.

Solution:

1. Write the invoice date		June 10
Add the extra days to the days allowed in the terms. 10 + 60 = 70. Add this amount to the invoice date.		+ 70
Date on which payment is due.		80
June does not have 80 days.		
Subtract the number of days in June.		− 30
July does not have 50 days.		50
Subtract the number of days in July.		− 31
Payment is due August 19.		19

2. Because of the extra days, payment is due August 19. There is no extension beyond the days for which the discount is allowed.

PRACTICE 2.5

A pet store purchases pet food for $520 on March 12. The terms are 2/10/N30. The store has bills for repairs and so the owner asks for extra time to pay without losing the discount. The vendor agrees to terms of 2/10–30X. Transportation is F.O.B. Store.

1. Who files insurance claims in case of damage to the goods during shipment?

2. Who pays transportation charges?

3. How much time do the new terms add to the discount period?

4. Find the last day for payment with the discount allowed.

5. Find the amount of the discount.

6. Find the amount due if payment is made during the discount period.

7. In the situation described above, at the buyer's request, the terms are changed to 2/10–60X. Determine the last date to make payment obtaining the cash discount.

A purchase of $350 is made with terms 3/10 E.O.M. The invoice is dated April 17. At the retailer's request the terms are changed to 3/10–60X.

8. Under the original terms, what is the last date for payment with the discount?

9. Under the revised terms, what is the last date for payment with the discount?

10. What is the dollar amount of the cash discount?

11. What amount is due if the invoice is paid on June 16?

CASH-ON-DELIVERY TERMS AND DATING

Suppliers frequently extend the time during which a discount is allowed in order to make sales and to keep customers. But if payment is delayed beyond allowable dates, or perhaps is not made in full, or if payment is not made at all, then suppliers will take a different approach. They will require that a retailer pay Cash-on-Delivery (C.O.D.). Unless otherwise stated, there is no cash discount given. The manufacturer regards the retailer as a poor credit risk and therefore insists upon immediate payment for the shipment, upon delivery. If the retailer is unable to pay for the shipment upon delivery, the shipment is returned to the manufacturer.

In some cases, purchases are made at the supplier's warehouse with payment at the time of sale. Terms in this case are similar to C.O.D., but the goods are not delivered. A transaction of this sort is called "Cash and Carry."

PRACTICE 2.6

A retailer purchases 100 dresses for $1,900, with terms C.O.D. The invoice is dated August 20, and delivery is made August 24.

1. When is payment due?

2. What discount is allowed?

A retailer orders 24 kitchen stools from a manufacturer's catalog. The catalog terms are 2/10/N30. After checking the retailer's credit, the manufacturer decides to ship the goods C.O.D. with a cash discount percent equal to the catalog terms. The 24 stools are delivered on October 5. The invoice amount is $300.

3. When is payment due?

4. What is the discount percent?

5. What is the dollar amount of the discount?

6. What is the amount to be paid?

A wholesaler operates a cash-and-carry business with terms of 2% for payment. A buyer purchases goods costing $500.

7. What is the dollar amount of the discount?

8. What amount must be paid?

9. Who has title to goods during transit?

10. Who pays transportation charges?

2.7 ON-MEMO OR ON-CONSIGNMENT TERMS AND DATING

Manufacturers burdened with unusually large inventory may offer goods to retailers with terms of "On-Memo" or "On-Consignment." With "On-Memo" terms, title to goods passes to the retailer at the point of origin.

When goods are on consignment, title is held by the supplier until the goods are actually sold. In this case the merchandise is really being lent to the store. This arrangement is, of course, advantageous to the retailer.

The retailer will try to include or negotiate the following in a consignment or memo arrangement:

The vendor pays all packing and transportation charges.

The vendor accepts return of all unsold merchandise.

The retailer pays only for goods that are sold.

The cost price and terms will be according to current market.

The schedule and final dates for return of goods will be agreed upon.

Example:

A manufacturer offers a retailer 1,000 pairs of slacks at $18 a pair with on-memo terms and an 8% cash discount. It is agreed that the retailer will accept shipment on April 1, and that the unsold portion will be returned on May 1. Six-hundred pairs of slacks are sold.

a. Who has title to the goods?

b. When should the retailer pay the manufacturer for the 600 pairs sold?

c. When should the 8% cash discount be deducted?

d. Who should pay for the transportation?

e. What amount must be paid?

Solution:

a. When goods are on memo, the retailer takes title at the supplier's warehouse.

b. Payment should be made shortly after May 1.

c. Discount is taken at the time of payment.

d. The retailer prefers that the manufacturer pay transportation, but this may be negotiated.

e.   The total amount sold, multiplied by the cost, is:

$$\$18 \times 600 = \$10,800.$$
$$\text{The discount is } \$10,800 \times 8\% = \$864.$$
$$\text{The amount to be paid is } \$10,800 - \$864 = \$9,936.$$

PRACTICE 2.7

A buyer purchases 2,000 blankets at $15 each on consignment. Delivery is to be made, F.O.B. Store, on August 1. The unsold portion is to be returned on September 1. Final payment for the purchase is to be made on October 1. The buyer requested and received a 2% cash discount. On the first of September, 1,382 blankets have been sold.

1. Who pays the transportation charges?

2. Who makes any claims regarding goods damaged while en route to the store?

3. How many blankets are returned?

4. What is the total cost of the blankets before discount?

5. When should payment be made?

6. What is the dollar amount of the discount?

7. What amount is to be paid?

A retailer purchases an order of 800 T-shirts at $4.50 each, on memo, F.O.B. factory, freight prepaid. The shirts are delivered on May 15. Unsold T-shirts are to be returned on September 1. Payment is due September 15. On September 1, 765 T-shirts have been sold.

8. Who pays the transportation charges?

9. Who has title to the goods while they are being transported?

10. What amount must be paid to the supplier for the T-shirts?

VOCABULARY REVIEW

Advance, Post, "As of":   Under "advance," "post," or "as of" terms, delivery of goods is made in advance of the invoice date.

Cash and Carry: Goods are purchased for cash and are taken by the buyer from the supplier's factory or warehouse.

Cash Discount: An amount subtracted from the supplier's invoice amount for payment within a certain time stated by the supplier.

C.O.D.:   Cash-on-Delivery, payment is required at the time of delivery.

E.O.M.:   End-of-Month, dating for discount begins on the last day of the month for which the invoice is dated.

Extra: A retailer receives an additional number of days in which to obtain the cash discount, for example, with the terms 2/10–X60, 60 days are added.

On-Memo or **On-Consignment:**   Goods are taken by the retailer under the terms that payment will not be until after the goods are sold and unsold goods may be returned to the supplier.

Ordinary Terms: These are terms that are commonly used in a particular industry.

R.O.G.:   Receipt-of-Goods, dating begins on the date of delivery.

CHAPTER TEST The following terms are stated on a vendor's invoice: 3/20/N30. The invoice is dated July 12.

1. What is the percent cash discount offered?

2. For how many days is the cash discount offered?

3. What is the meaning of N30?

4. What is the last day for paying the invoice?

An invoice contains the terms 3/30/2/45. It is dated March 18.

5. What percent discount is allowed if the invoice is paid on April 18?

6. What percent discount is allowed if payment is made on May 20?

7. What is the last day for which a 2% discount can be obtained?

Electronics, Inc., sells an order of compact disks and cassette tapes to The Listener's Shop. The invoice is dated August 21. The amount of the invoice is $946. The cash discount terms are 5/30/4/60.

8. Find the last date for which a 5% discount is allowed.

9. What percent discount is allowed if the invoice is paid on October 2?

10. What is the dollar amount of the discount if the invoice is paid on October 2?

11. What amount must be paid on October 2?

A purchase of $2,505 has an invoice date of November 14 with terms 8/10 E.O.M.

12. What is the last date for which the discount is allowed?

13. What is the dollar amount of the discount?

14. What is the amount of payment if the invoice is paid December 8?

A buyer purchases merchandise on May 1. He wants to receive the goods on July 1. The supplier offers to date the invoice July 15 if the buyer will accept the shipment on June 1. The terms are 2/10/N30. The invoice amount is $4,600.

15. Determine the last date to make payment and to obtain the cash discount.

16. Determine the last date to make payment without the cash discount.

17. Determine the invoice amount if payment is made on July 21.

A building supply store is having problems because of an economic recession. The owner purchases cement and cinder blocks under terms 2/10–X60. The invoice is dated March 10. The amount of the invoice is $1,566.

18. What is the last day for which the cash discount is allowed?

19. What is the amount of the discount in dollars?

20. What is the amount if the invoice is paid within the discount period?

A buyer purchases 3,000 frying pans at $8 each on consignment. Goods are to be accepted, F.O.B., Factory on September 1. The unsold portion is to be returned on November 1. Final payment for the purchase is to be made on December 1. The buyer requested and received a 1% cash discount. On the first of November, 2,400 frying pans have been sold.

21. Who pays the transportation charges?

22. What is the total cost of the fry pans before discount?

23. When should payment be made?

24. What is the dollar amount of the discount?

25. What amount is to be paid?

ANSWERS

2.1
1. 3%
2. 20 days
3. The invoice is to be paid within 30 days.
4. 10 days
5. July 1
6. 30 days
7. July 21
8. 4%
9. 3%
10. May 11
11. May 21
12. 3%
13. 2%
14. 2%
15. September 27
16. October 27
17. November 26

2.2
1. March 20
2. 5%
3. $120.96
4. $2,903.04
5. Xavier Publishing Co.
6. When they are delivered to the store
7. $18.24
8. $893.76
9. $912
10. May 4

2.3
1. October 10
2. $147.60
3. $1,328.40
4. June 20
5. July 10
6. Home Beauty Store
7. 2%
8. $2,303.98
9. Hanover Store
10. ABX Company
11. $39.12
12. $938.88
13. $978
14. $929.10
15. The supplier, The Running Co.
16. The retailer, The Athlete's World pays the freight and deducts the amount from the invoice.

17. $587.50, deducting the freight charge
18. 2%
19. $11.75
20. $575.75

2.4
1. April 11
2. $26.80
3. $1,340
4. June 25
5. July 15
6. $544.17
7. January 10
8. $81.60
9. October 25
10. $762.42
11. The retailer
12. The retailer
13. 2%
14. $11.96
15. $586.04
16. October 20
17. $187.20
18. $2,152.80
19. The supplier
20. The retailer

2.5
1. The supplier
2. The supplier
3. 30 days
4. April 21
5. $10.40
6. $509.60
7. May 21
8. May 10
9. June 26
10. $10.50
11. $339.50

2.6
1. August 24
2. None
3. October 5
4. 2%
5. $6
6. $294
7. $10
8. $490

9. The retailer
10. The retailer

2.7 1. The supplier
2. The supplier
3. 618
4. $20,730
5. October 1
6. $414.60
7. $20,315.40
8. The supplier
9. The retailer
10. $3,442.50

CHAPTER TEST

1. 3%

2. 20 days

3. The invoice amount must be paid within 30 days.

4. August 11

5. 2%

6. No discount available

7. May 2

8. September 20

9. 4%

10. $37.84

11. $908.16

12. December 10

13. $200.40

14. $2,304.60

15. July 25

16. August 14

17. $4,508

18. May 19

19. $31.32
20. $1,534.68
21. The retailer
22. $19,200
23. December 1
24. $192
25. $19,008

3 Discounts

In Chapter 2 the terms used to calculate cash discounts were explained. These terms determine the percent and dollar amounts of discounts as well as the number of days during which different discounts are allowed. We also calculated discount amounts and the amount of payment due after taking a discount.

In this chapter other kinds of discounts are presented, including the reasons for discounts, different methods to calculate discount amounts, and how discounts may affect sales and profits.

After completing this chapter you will be able to:

- Explain the different reasons for which discounts are given.
- Calculate discount amounts and payment due.
- Calculate multiple discounts and payment due.

THE REASONS FOR DISCOUNTS

Suppliers offer discounts for various reasons:

To encourage early payment,

To encourage early buying,

To encourage large purchase quantities,

To encourage retailers to sell the supplier's product,

To adjust the supplier's prices to meet fluctuations in raw materials.

Retailers who take advantage of discounts will reduce their costs and increase profits. But discounts should not lead retailers to purchase more than they can sell. This would lead to waste and losses rather than profits.

Retailers also offer discounts to customers. Most retailers offer employee discounts. Some offer discounts for large purchases and some provide discounts to those involved with charitable work.

Rounding is an important skill when working with numbers. The following example shows how to round two numbers.

Example:

a. Round $4,781,526.39 to the nearest dollar.

b. Round $4,781,526.39 to the nearest thousand dollars.

Solution:

a. The number 4,781,526.39 has 6 in the units (or dollar) place. Looking at the digit to the right of 6, we find 3. 3 is less than 5, so we leave the 6 unchanged. The number rounded is $4,781,526.

b. The number 4,781,526.39 has 1 in the thousands place. Looking at the digit to the right of the 1, we find 5. 5 is "5 or greater," so we increase the 1 to 2. The number rounded to the nearest thousand dollars is $4,782,000. We have supplied 0s as needed.

3.1 CASH DISCOUNTS

Retailers often debate the question, "Is the cash discount a reward for paying on time or a penalty for paying late?" Suppliers undoubtedly consider the cash discount an incentive for early payment. Retailers, short of funds, might consider the cash discount a penalty. In fact, taking advantage of the cash discount serves a variety of purposes and can be used to benefit both buyer and seller.

In Chapter 2 the method for calculating cash discounts included several steps:

1. Change the percent to a decimal;

2. Multiply the invoice amount by the decimal to find the discount amount;

3. Subtract the discount amount from the invoice amount to find the payment needed.

There is a shorter way to find the payment amount that is particularly efficient when using a calculator. It is called the complementary method. If, for example, a 10% discount is applied to an invoice, the amount to be paid is 90% of the original invoice. Therefore, the payment amount could have been determined by taking 90% of the invoice.

Example:

An invoice of $1,200 is given a cash discount of 8%.

a. Use the subtraction method to find the payment amount.

b. Use the complementary method to find the payment amount.

Solution:

a. 8% = 0.08

$$1,200 \times 0.08 = 96$$
$$1,200 - 96 = 1,104$$

The payment amount is $1,104.

b. The complement of 8% is 92%, since $100 - 8 = 92$.

$$92\% = 0.92$$
$$1,200 \times 0.92 = 1,104$$

The payment amount is $1,104.

PRACTICE 3.1

Use the complementary method in the following problems, unless you are asked to find the discount amount.

A purchase is made for $978. The invoice date is July 12 and cash discount terms are 5/15/4/30/3/60.

1. What is the complement of the first discount percent?

2. What is the last date to gain the first discount?

3. Find the payment amount allowing the first discount.

4. Find the payment amount if payment is made on September 5.

5. Find the amount if payment is made on August 3.

A purchase costing $3,060 is made on September 20. Transportation terms are F.O.B. Factory. Cash discount terms are 3/30/N60.

6. Who pays the transportation charges?

7. What is the last date for which the discount is allowed?

8. What is the amount if payment is made on October 4?

A retailer places an order for $850 for running shoes. Delivery is made on June 15. The terms are 8/10 E.O.M.

9. What is the last date for payment that will allow the discount?

10. What is the amount if payment is made during the discount period?

The cost price of a purchase is $3,500. Delivery is made on February 20. The terms are 2/10 as of April 1.

11. Find the last day for which the discount is allowed.

12. Find the dollar amount of the discount.

13. Find the amount if payment is made within the discount period.

A retailer makes a cash and carry purchase for $375 with a 2% discount.

14. Who pays for the transportation of the goods?

15. What is the amount of payment with the discount?

3.2 TRADE DISCOUNT

In some industries, such as the lumber industry, prices fluctuate. Raw materials that are used to build houses or to manufacture furniture can vary almost from day to day.

A manufacturer sets prices to retailers by:

1. stating a base or list price;

2. including one or several trade discounts. If the manufacturer's cost increases, fewer discounts are offered.

Several discounts are called a *Series of Discounts* or *Functional Discounts*. These may be used to compensate the retailer for saving the supplier money by paying for delivery or advertising, or for special promotional activities. Trade discounts are sometimes written, for example, $100 less 10, 10, 5.

The complementary method is especially well suited for calculating a series of discounts.

Example:

An order for $450 is purchased with trade discounts of 10%, 10%, and 5%. Find the amount to be paid after taking the discounts.

Solution:

The complement of 10% is 90%. The complement of 5% is 95%. To find the payment amount multiply: $450 \times 90\% \times 90\% \times 95\%$. In decimal form multiply: $450 \times 0.90 \times 0.90 \times 0.95 = 346.275$. Rounded to the nearest cent, the amount to be paid is $346.28.

PRACTICE 3.2

1. An item with a manufacturer's list price of $100 contains trade discounts of 10% and 10%. Find the retailer's price after the discounts are taken.

2. A manufacturer offers terms of $200, less 10, 10. Find the cost price to the retailer.

The following items show manufacturers' prices and trade discount terms. Find the prices after taking the discounts that are listed. Round each answer to the nearest cent.

3. $78 less 10, 10.

4. $398.50, less 10, 10, 5.

5. $876.70 less 10, 5.

6. $1,246.35 less 10, 10, 5.

7. $542 less 10, 5, 3.

8. $895.74 less 10, 5, 3.

3.3   TRADE AND CASH DISCOUNTS

To encourage prompt payment, manufacturers often include both trade and cash discounts. Once again, the complementary method is well suited to the calculation of payment. It is, of course, important to read the terms carefully to determine whether the cash discount applies.

Example:

A retailer orders a shipment of lumber of various sizes. The invoice is for $1,256 with trade discounts of 10%, 10%. Cash discount terms are 1/15 E.O.M. The invoice is dated February 21.

a. Find the last day of payment with the cash discount.

b. Find the amount of payment with the trade discounts but not the cash discount.

c. Find the amount of payment with all discounts allowed.

Solution:

a. The last date for discount is 15 days after the end of the month, that is, March 15.

b. $1{,}256 \times 0.9 \times 0.9 = 1{,}017.36$.

c. $1{,}256 \times 0.9 \times 0.9 \times 0.99 = 1{,}007.1864$.

Rounded, the payment with all discounts is $1,007.19.

PRACTICE 3.3

1. A manufacturer quotes a list price of $200 with trade discounts of 10%, 5%, and a cash discount of 1%. Find the amount of payment with all discounts taken.

A manufacturer quotes trade discount terms of 10%, 10%, 2%, and a cash discount of 1%. Terms are C.O.D. The invoice for $873.29 is dated June 10. Delivery is made on June 15.

2. Who has title to the goods while they are being shipped?

3. Who pays the transportation charges?

4. On what date is payment due?

5. How much should be paid, assuming all discounts?

6. What is likely to happen if payment is not made on the pre-scribed date?

A manufacturer's catalog quotes the following prices for a metal fence: $575 less 10, 5, 2, 1. Cash discount terms are 2/10/N30 R.O.G. A retailer makes a purchase according to these terms. The date of the invoice is

May 5. The delivery date is May 10. Transportation charges are: F.O.B. Store, Charges Reversed.

7. Who makes claims if there are any damages to the goods during shipment?

8. Who finally pays the transportation charges?

9. What is the amount to be paid if payment is made on May 16?

10. What is the amount to be paid if payment is made on June 1?

3.4 QUANTITY DISCOUNTS

Manufacturers frequently offer lower prices for the purchase of a large quantity of a product. In fact, the larger the quantity purchased, the lower the price is likely to be.

The manufacturer effects savings when purchasing raw materials in large quantities and will pass along some of these savings to the retailer. The retailer can pass savings along to the customer.

It is not, however, a good business practice for a retailer to purchase a larger quantity than needed in order to obtain a lower unit price. Losses caused by lack of sales and surplus inventory can be great.

A manufacturer's price list might read as follows:

1–249 items	@$5.00
250–499 items	@$4.50
500–999 items	@$4.00
1,000+ items	@$3.50

A retailer who is able to buy 1,000 items at a time will have a competitive edge over a retailer who can only buy 500 items at a time. Fifty cents might not seem like a lot. But customers notice when the prices in one store are consistently lower than those in a competing store. Consumers understand that small savings on a number of items add up to substantial overall savings.

Quantity discounts may be calculated along with trade and cash discounts using the complementary method.

Example:

A manufacturer's price list reads as follows:

$$1–499 \text{ items}\quad @\$1.00$$

$$500–1,000 \text{ items}\quad @\$0.90$$

$$1,000+ \text{ items}\quad @\$0.70$$

with trade discounts of 10%, 10%, and a cash discount of 1%.

   a. Find the list price of 500 items.

   b. Find the amount to be paid for 500 items, allowing all discounts.

Solution:

   a. 500 @ $0.90: $500 \times 0.90 = \$450$.

   b. $500 \times 0.90 \times 0.90 \times 0.99 = 360.855$.

Rounded to the nearest cent, the payment amount is $360.86.

PRACTICE 3.4

A manufacturer offers a list price of $10, less 10, and 10, with a cash discount of 2% for immediate payment. For a purchase of 200 items or more the price is $9 with the same discounts.

   1. Find the total list price for 150 items.

   2. Find the payment for 150 items with all discounts taken.

   3. Find the payment for 200 items with trade discounts but no cash discount.

   4. Find the payment for 250 items with all discounts.

A manufacturer sells shirts for $10 each. He offers a quantity discount of 10% if the retailer purchases 100. The cash discount terms are 2/10/N30. The transportation terms are F.O.B., Destination.

5. Who pays the transportation charges?

6. What is the amount of payment for 100 shirts with allowable discounts?

A manufacturer's price list for pocket calculators reads as follows:

1–249 items   @$9.00

250–499 items   @$8.50

500–999 items   @$8.00

1,000+ items   @$7.00

Trade discounts of 10% and 5% are offered, as well as cash discount terms of 2/10/N30.

7. Find the cost price of 1,500 calculators with all discounts.

8. A retailer purchases 300 calculators. The invoice for the sale is dated January 25. She pays the bill on February 6. Find the amount of payment.

9. A retailer buys 600 calculators. The invoice is dated February 21. What amount is due if he pays on February 27?

10. Find the cost of 90 calculators with all discounts.

CHAPTER TEST

A retailer purchases office supplies with an invoice for $2,573, dated June 20. The cash discount terms are 4/15/3/30/2/60. The transportation terms are F.O.B. Factory.

1. What is the complement of the first percent offered?

2. What is the last date to gain the first discount?

3. Find the payment amount allowing the first discount.

4. Find the payment amount if payment is made on July 25.

5. Who pays transportation charges?

Numbers 6–8 show manufacturers' prices and trade discount terms. Find each amount due after trade discounts are taken.

6. $7,600 less 10, 10.

7. $21,600 less 10, 10, 5.

8. $9,674.20 less 10, 5, 3.

A manufacturer quotes trade discount terms of 10%, 5%, 2%, and cash discount terms of 2/10/R.O.G. The invoice for $4,050 is dated August 24. Delivery is made on August 29. Transportation terms are F.O.B. Store.

9. Who has title to the goods while they are being shipped?

10. Who pays the transportation charges?

11. What is the last date for payment with all discounts?

12. What is the amount, if payment is made on September 5?

A manufacturer's price list reads as follows:

1–499 items @$12.00

500–999 items @$11.00

1,000+ items @$ 9.50

with trade discounts of 10%, 5%, and 3%, and cash discount terms of 1/10 E.O.M.

13. Find the amount due for an order of 600 items with all discounts allowed.

14. A purchase of 1,200 items is made with an invoice dated October 12. Find the amount, if payment is made on November 4.

A retailer purchases 400 items according to the prices and terms listed above, with transportation terms F.O.B. Store, Charges Reversed.

15. Find the cost of the items before any discount is taken.

16. Who finally pays the transportation charges?

17. Who has title to the goods during transit?

18. What is the charge if trade discounts are allowed but the cash discount is not allowed because of late payment?

19. What is the amount if all discounts are allowed?

20. What must be paid for an order of 500 items with all discounts?

ANSWERS

3.1
1. 95%
2. July 27
3. $929.10
4. $948.66
5. $938.88
6. The retailer
7. October 20
8. $2,968.20
9. July 10
10. $782
11. April 11
12. $70
13. $3,430
14. The retailer
15. $367.50

3.2
1. $81
2. $162
3. $63.18
4. $306.65
5. $749.58
6. $959.07
7. $449.51
8. $742.88

3.3
1. $169.29
2. The supplier
3. The supplier
4. June 15
5. $686.29
6. The goods will be taken back to the supplier.
7. The supplier
8. The retailer
9. $467.44
10. $476.97

3.4
1. $1,500
2. $1,190.70
3. $1,458
4. $1,786.05
5. The supplier
6. $882
7. $8,797.95
8. $2,180.25
9. $4,021.92
10. $678.70

CHAPTER TEST

1. 96%
2. July 5
3. $2,470.08
4. $2,521.54
5. The retailer
6. $6,156
7. $16,621.20
8. $8,023.30
9. The supplier
10. The supplier
11. September 8
12. $3,325.63
13. $5,418.97
14. $9,360.04
15. $4,800
16. The retailer
17. The supplier
18. $3,980.88
19. $3,941.07
20. $4,515.81

4 Markon Based on Selling Price

A retail store owner buys products in large quantities, then sells the products one at a time or in small quantities. Suppose, for example, you own a store that sells athletic shoes. You buy hundreds of pairs of shoes of different kinds and sizes. Then, to make money, you sell the shoes at prices higher than you paid for them.

After completing this chapter you will be able to:

- Explain the use of markon based on selling price.

- Calculate the markon amount when markon percent is given.

- Explain and use the markon equations, based on selling price, in dollars and in percent.

- Calculate markon, markon percent, selling price, cost, and cost percent when given sufficient information.

4.1 THE MARKON EQUATIONS

The amount that a retailer adds to the cost in order to establish a retail selling price is called *markon*.

$$\text{Cost} + \text{Markon} = \text{Selling Price}$$

Markup is an amount added to the original selling price to give a new, higher selling price. In practice, markon and markup are often used interchangeably. Markon is sometimes called initial markup. The same equations and mathematical procedures are used whether you are working with markon or markup.

The *cost* of an item to the retailer includes: the supplier's price; the transportation charges, if they are paid by the store; prepackaging charges; labeling charges; certain taxes paid by the store; other minor charges. In general, the cost is what the retail owner pays the supplier for the items purchased.

The *selling price* is what the store charges for an item; it is the amount that the purchaser pays.

A retail store owner must pay *expenses,* such as: payroll for employees; rent for the store; heat and light bills; insurance; advertising; telephone.

In addition to paying for expenses, retailers expect to earn money for themselves. This amount beyond what is needed to pay expenses is called *profit.* Profit is included when the retailer calculates his or her selling price. Therefore, profit as well as expenses are included in the markon amount.

We return now to the markon equation:

$$\text{Cost} + \text{Markon} = \text{Selling Price}$$

If two terms of this equation are known, the third term can be found.

Example:

A coat costs a retailer $60; it is then sold for $100. Find the amount of markon.

$$60 + \text{Markon} = 100$$
$$\text{Markon} = 100 - 60 = 40$$

The amount of markon is $40.

Example:

A TV costing the retailer $120 receives a $70 markon. Find the selling price.

$$120 + 70 = \text{Selling Price}$$
$$190 = \text{Selling Price}$$

The selling price is $190.

PRACTICE 4.1

Use the markon equation to solve each of the following:

1. A chair costing $40 is sold for $75. Find the markon amount.

2. The selling price of a sweater is $39. It received a markon of $10. What was the cost to the retailer?

3. A lamp costs the retailer $45. She adds a markon of $20. Find the selling price.

4. A book sells for $19.95. It has a markon of $8.50. Find the retailer's cost.

5. A box of cereal costs the retail store $2.80 and sells for $4.20. What is the markon amount?

4.2 FINDING MARKON AMOUNT AND SELLING PRICE

The triangle shown in Figure 4–1 can help you solve percent problems. The markon percent is p; the amount, a, is the markon amount; the base, b, is the selling price. When you know the percent and the selling price, you multiply to find the markon amount. The percent and selling price are adjacent. This will help you remember to multiply. When you know the markon amount and either the percent or the selling price, then you

FIGURE 4–1

divide to find the missing term. The horizontal line will help you remember which numbers to divide.

Example:

A computer received a markon of 40%, which amounted to $280. Find the selling price and the cost of the computer.

Solution:

Markon Amount = Markon Percent × Selling Price
280   =   40%   × Selling Price

To find the selling price, divide both sides of the equation by 40%.

Selling Price = 280 ÷ 40%
= 280 ÷ 0.4
= 700

To find the cost, subtract the markon from the selling price.

700 − 280 = 420

The cost is $420.

In the following practice problems, any of three dollar amounts might be found. They are: cost, markon, and selling price. But the markon percent equation contains only markon and selling price. So you must be careful to find and use the correct amounts.

PRACTICE 4.2

Running shoes that cost $40 are sold for $80.

1. Find the markon amount.

2. Find the markon percent.

A hat selling for $15 had received a markon of 60%.

  3. Find the markon amount.

  4. Find the cost.

A calculator has a markon of 40% and a markon amount of $48.

  5. Find the selling price.

  6. Find the cost.

A car sells for $11,000. It cost the dealer $9,000.

  7. Find the markon amount.

  8. Find the markon percent.

4.3 FINDING MARKON WHEN COST AND SELLING PRICE ARE GIVEN

We have seen that markon is a percent of selling price. We also know that cost and markon add up to selling price. Finally, we know that the whole of something is one hundred percent (100%). Therefore, we can now see that the markon equation is valid for percent as well as for dollar amount.

Example:

You purchase an item for $15. The cost to the store is $7. Find (a) the markon amount, (b) the markon percent, (c) the cost percent.

Solution:

  a.
$$\text{Cost} + \text{Markon} = \text{Selling Price}$$
$$\$7 + \text{Markon} = \$15$$

Therefore, the markon amount is $8.

b. Markon Amount = Markon Percent × Selling Price
    8   = Markon Percent ×   15
Markon Percent   = 8 ÷ 15
                   = 0.533
                   = 53.3%

c.   Cost % + Markon % = Selling Price %
            Cost % +   53.3% =   100%

Therefore, the cost percent is $100 - 53.3 = 46.7$. The cost is 46.7% of the selling price.

PRACTICE 4.3

A video selling for $12 was purchased by the store for $7.

1. Find the markon amount.

2. Find the markon percent.

3. Find the cost as a percent of the selling price.

A chair sells for $190. It has received a markon of 60%.

4. Find the markon amount.

5. Find the cost as a percent of the selling price.

6. Find the cost to the store.

A sweater selling for $39 received a markon of $15.

7. Find the cost to the store.

8. Find the markon percent.

9. Find the cost as a percent of the selling price.

A box of cereal sells for $4.25. The cost to the store is 55% of the selling price.

10. Find the markon percent.

11. Find the markon amount.

12. Find the cost.

CHAPTER TEST   Match each term in the left-hand column by writing the letter for its definition from the right-hand column.

1. Markon   _____   a. parts out of one hundred

2. Expenses   _____   b. the difference between selling price and cost

3. Profit   _____   c. what the retailer pays for an item

4. Selling price   _____   d. amounts, separate from the cost of merchandise, that must be paid to run a business

5. Percent   _____   e. what the customer pays for an item

6. Cost   _____   f. the amount that a business earns after paying the cost of merchandise and expenses

As the owner of a sporting goods store, you purchase 100 T-shirts for $400.

7.   What is your cost per item for the T-shirts?

You sell the T-shirts for $8.50 each.

8.   What is the markon amount per T-shirt?

9.   What is the markon percent per T-shirt?

10.   What is the cost percent per T-shirt?

11.   What will be the total sales if you sell all the T-shirts?

You are selling XL cross-trainer athletic shoes for $75 a pair. They have received a 45% markon.

12.   What is the markon amount?

13.   What is the cost to the retailer?

14.   What is the cost as a percent of the selling price?

You buy jackets for $48. You give them a markon of $18.

15.   Find the markon percent.

16.   Find the cost.

17.   Find the cost as a percent of the selling price.

You sell sweatshirts for $18. The cost is 60% of selling price.

18. Find the markon as a percent of the selling price.

19. Find the markon amount.

20. Find the cost.

ANSWERS

4.1
1. $35
2. $29
3. $65
4. $11.45
5. $1.40

4.2
1. $40
2. 50%
3. $9
4. $6
5. $120
6. $72
7. $2,000
8. 18.2%

4.3
1. $5
2. 41.7%
3. 58.3%
4. $114
5. 40%
6. $76
7. $24
8. 38.5%
9. 61.5%
10. 45%
11. $1.91
12. $2.34

CHAPTER TEST

1. b
2. d
3. f
4. e
5. a
6. c
7. $4
8. $4.50
9. 53%

10. 47%
11. $850
12. $33.75
13. $41.25
14. 55%
15. 37.5%
16. $30
17. 62.5%
18. 40%
19. $7.20
20. $10.80

5 Markon Based on Cost Price

Although many retailers base markon and markon percent on the selling price of an item, others use their cost price as the base. Some retailers carry and sell a small number of high-priced items, such as specialty gifts, automobiles, or jewelry. The prices for such items are sometimes negotiable and are often subject to discounts. Some retailers, consequently, prefer to maintain markon records based on cost, rather than selling price.

After completing this chapter you will be able to:

- Explain the calculations of markon based on cost price.

- Use the Markon Equation to make calculations based on cost price.

- Solve practical problems to find cost, markon, and selling price as well as percents of each, when sufficient information is given.

- Explain the use of vendor advertising related to markon based on cost price.

5.1 THE MARKON EQUATION

In addition to the chain stores that carry many items of the same type, there are, at the other extreme of retail business, specialty stores that carry unusual or one-of-a-kind items. Antique stores and certain gift stores fit into this category. Those who own and operate stores of this kind are conscious of an item's cost and try to establish selling prices that will bring the profit they need. Stores of this type are likely to use a cost-based method when considering markon.

The markon equation is the same as the equation presented in Chapter 4. But all percent calculations will be different because the base is now cost rather than selling price. That is, the cost is 100% and the selling price is more than 100%.

Cost + Markon = Selling Price

If a retailer purchases desk calculators for $90 and establishes a selling price of $135, then the markon equation, in dollars and percent, will be as follows:

Cost + Markon = Selling Price
$90 + $45   = $135
100% +   50%   =   150%

FINDING MARKON AMOUNT, COST, AND SELLING PRICE

When calculating percent or dollar amounts based on the cost price, you can use the same triangle that was used in Chapter 4 (see Figure 5–1). But it is important to remember that the base is the cost price.

FIGURE 5–1

Example 1:

An item is purchased by a retailer for $1,000 and sold at a 50% markon.

    a. Find the amount of markon.

    b. Find the selling price.

Solution:

Use the markon equation: Cost + Markon = Selling Price

    a. Using the percent triangle, the base (cost) and rate (percent) are next to each other. Therefore, multiply to find the markon amount.

$$1,000 \times 0.50 = 500$$

or, using the markon percent equation:

$$\text{Markon Amount} = \text{Cost} \times \text{Markon Percent}$$
$$= 1,000 \times 50\% = 500$$

The markon amount is $500.

    b. Adding markon to cost: 1,000 + 500 = 1,500

The selling price is $1,500.

Example 2:

A chair receives a markon of $270 by a retailer. This is 90% of the retailer's cost price. Find the cost and selling price.

Solution:

    a. Using the percent triangle, the markon amount is over the rate. Therefore, divide to find the cost.

$$270 \div 0.90 = 300$$

or, using the markon percent equation,

$$\text{Markon Amount} = \text{Cost} \times \text{Markon Percent}$$
$$\text{Cost} = \text{Markon Amount/Markon Percent}$$
$$= 270/0.90 = 300$$

The cost price is $300.

b. Adding markon to cost: $300 + 270 = 570$

The selling price is $570.

PRACTICE 5.1

An antique dealer purchases a table for $800. She applies 50% markon based on the cost price.

  1. Find the markon amount.

  2. Find the selling price.

A convenience store owner orders soap and adds a markon of $0.84, which is 60% of the cost price.

  3. Find the cost.

  4. Find the selling price.

An item receives a 40% of cost markon, which amounts to $80.

  5. Find the cost price.

  6. Find the selling price.

A large supermarket receives a shipment of 100 cases of canned tomatoes. Each case contains 12 cans. The goods are shipped F.O.B., Store. The invoice amount is $540. The goods receive a markon of 60% of the cost price.

  7. Who pays the transportation charges?

  8. How many cans are delivered?

9. What is the cost price per can?

10. Find the markon amount per can.

11. Find the selling price per can.

A retailer who owns a chain of gift stores places an order for 20 dozen picture frames. The transportation terms are F.O.B. Factory. The discount terms are 2/10 R.O.G. The invoice amount for $1,200 is dated March 3. The goods are delivered on March 15. A markon of 90% of cost price is added per picture frame.

12. How many picture frames are purchased?

13. Who pays the transportation charges?

14. Who has title to the goods while they are being transported?

15. What is the last day for which the cash discount is allowed?

16. What is the amount of payment if the invoice is paid on March 20?

17. Find the cost per picture frame after deducting the discount.

18. Find the amount of markon per picture frame.

19. Find the selling price.

An antique lamp receives a total markon of $280, which is 70% of cost.

20. Find the cost price.

21. Find the selling price for the lamp.

22. Find the selling price as a percent of the cost.

5.2 FINDING COST AND MARKON WHEN SELLING PRICE AND PERCENT ARE GIVEN

The percent triangle and percent equation can be used in different situations. You have seen that if a markon is 40% of the cost, then, using the cost as base, the selling price will be 140% of cost. Knowing this, we can write an equation that connects the cost and selling price.

Cost × Selling Price as Percent of Cost = Selling Price

This means that if you know, or can find out, the value of any two terms in this equation, you can find the third term. In this section you will determine selling price and cost when percents are given.

Example:

The retail price of an item is $400. This is 200% of the cost price.

   a. Find the cost price.

   b. Find the markon amount.

Solution:

   a. Substituting in the cost/percent equation:

Cost × Selling Price as Percent of Cost = Selling Price
Cost × 200% = 400
Cost × 2.00 = 400, changing 200% to a decimal

To solve this equation, divide both sides by 2.00

400 ÷ 2.00 = 200

The cost price is $200

   b. To find the markon: 400 − 200 = 200

The markon amount is $200.

PRACTICE 5.2

A retail price is $300. The retail price is 150% of the cost price.

   1. Find the cost price.

   2. Find the markon amount.

A retail price is $480. The markon percent of cost is 60%.

   3. Find the retail price as a percent of cost.

   4. Find the cost price.

   5. Find the markon amount.

A retail price of $116 represents 145% of cost.

   6. Find the cost price.

   7. Find the markon amount.

   8. Find the markon as a percent of cost.

5.3 CALCULATING PERCENTS

We have used the percent equation (and the percent triangle) to calculate the markon, cost, and selling price. This method can also be used to calculate markon percent, when any two of the three amounts (cost, markon, and selling price) are known.

Example:

An item is purchased for $125 and is sold for $190.

   a. Find the amount of markon.

   b. Find the markon percent based on cost.

Solution:

   a. Markon = Selling Price − Cost
      Markon = 190 − 125 = 65

   b. Cost × Markon Percent = Markon Amount
      Markon Percent = Markon Amount ÷ Cost
      Markon Percent = 65 ÷ 125 = 0.52

The markon percent is 52%.

PRACTICE 5.3

A chair is purchased for $550 and is sold for $770.

 1. Find the markon amount.

 2. Find the markon as a percent of cost.

A piano is bought for $1,200. It is sold for $660 more than the purchase price.

 3. Find the selling price.

 4. Find the markon as a percent of cost.

A shipment of 500 tubes of toothpaste is purchased at $0.89 cents a tube. Each tube is then sold for $1.49.

 5. Find the markon amount for each tube.

 6. Find the markon percent, rounded to the nearest percent.

 7. Find the cost to the retailer of the 500 tubes.

 8. Find the revenue, that is, the total amount of money received, if all 500 tubes are sold.

 9. Find the amount of profit, that is, the difference between the amount paid to the retailer and the cost to the retailer, if all 500 tubes are sold.

A retailer purchases 200 sweaters for $3,000. The sweaters are delivered F.O.B. Store, Charges Reversed. Cash discount terms are 2/10 E.O.M. The invoice is dated August 2. The order is delivered on August 7. The retailer establishes a sales price of $24.

 10. Find the cost price per sweater.

 11. Find the last day for which the cash discount is allowed.

 12. Find the amount to be paid if payment is made within the discount period.

 13. Who finally pays the transportation charges?

14. Who has title to the goods while they are being transported?

15. What is the amount of markon, not considering the cash discount?

16. What is the markon as a percent of cost, not considering the cash discount?

5.4 CONVERTING BETWEEN MARKON BASED ON COST AND ON SELLING PRICE

Manufacturers and manufacturers' representatives (sales reps) tend to express markon as a percentage of cost. Because cost is lower than selling price, this method always gives a higher percentage than using the selling price as a base.

Recall the general percent equation:

$$\text{Rate} \times \text{Base} = \text{Amount}$$

When calculating markon, this equation is:

$$\text{Markon Percent} \times \text{Base} = \text{Markon Amount}$$

and

$$\text{Markon Percent} = \text{Markon Amount/Base}$$

Example 1:

An item costs a retailer $2 and is sold for $3. Thus, the markon is $1.

a. Find the markon percent based on cost.

b. Find the markon percent based on selling price.

Solution:

a. Using the cost as a base: Markon Percent = 1/2 = 0.50 = 50%

b. Using the selling price as a base: Markon Percent = 1/3 = 0.33 = 33%

Example 2:

An item is marked up $3.60, which is 45% of the cost price.

    a. Find the cost price.

    b. Find the selling price.

    c. Find the markon percent based on the selling price.

Solution:

    a.   Cost = Markon ÷ Markon Percent
            Cost = 3.60 ÷ 0.45 = $8.00

    b.   Cost + Markon = Selling Price
            8.00 + 3.60 = 11.60

    c.   Markon Percent = Markon ÷ Selling Price
            Markon Percent = 3.60 ÷ 11.60 = 0.31 = 31%

PRACTICE 5.4

In the following exercises 1–5, find the markon percent based on cost (a) and based on selling price (b).

    1. An item is purchased for $10 and is sold for $18.

    2. A table is purchased for $20 and is sold for $40.

    3. Soap is purchased for $1.50 a bar and is sold for $3.00 a bar.

    4. A TV is purchased for $80 and is sold for $140.

    5. Shirts are purchased for $7.85 and are sold for $12.95.

A retailer purchases coats for $50 and adds a 60% markon based on cost.

    6. Find the amount of markon.

    7. Find the selling price.

    8. Find the markon percent based on the selling price.

A retailer sells a computer for $360. There is a 60% markon based on selling price.

9. Find the amount of markon.

10. Find the cost.

11. Find the percent of markon based on cost.

An item receives a markon of $1.70, which is 25% of cost.

12. Find the cost.

13. Find the selling price.

14. Find the markon as a percent of selling price.

An item receives a markon of $336 and is sold at a price of $896.

15. Find the cost.

16. Find the markon percent based on cost.

17. Find the markon percent based on selling price.

5.5   CONVERTING DIRECTLY BETWEEN PERCENT BASED ON COST AND ON SELLING PRICE

It is possible to convert directly between markon percent based on cost and based on selling price. It is important to remember with which base you are beginning. If, for example, you want to convert a markon of 100% based on cost to a markon percent based on selling price, you can use the equation that follows. Note that since the markon percent is based on cost, the cost is 100%.

$$\text{Cost \%} + \text{Markon \%} = \text{Selling Price \%}$$
$$100\% + 100\% = 200\%$$

Since the ratio of markon amount to selling price is proportional to the ratio of markon percent to selling price percent, we have:

$$\text{Markon \% = Markon amount/Selling price}$$
$$\text{= Markon \%/Selling Price \%}$$

We do not know the markon amount or selling price amount and so we go directly to the ratio for percents.

$$\text{Markon \% = 100\%/200\% = 0.5 = 50\%}$$

Therefore, a markon of 100% of cost equals a markon on 50% of selling price.

In order to convert a markon as percent of selling price to percent of cost, we consider selling price as 100%. For example, a markon of 40% of selling means that the cost itself represents 60% of selling price and the following equation can be written:

$$\text{Cost \% + Markon \% = Selling Price \%}$$
$$\text{60\% + 40\% = 100\%}$$

We can again use the ratio for percents.

$$\text{Markon \% = 40\%/60\% ≈ 67\%}$$

PRACTICE 5.5

1. An item receives a markon of 25% of cost. Find the markon as a percent of the selling price.

2. An item receives a markon of 75% of cost. Find the markon as a percent of the selling price.

3. An item receives a markon of 40% of the selling price. Find the markon as a percent of cost.

4. An item receives a markon of 60% of the selling price. Find the markon as a percent of cost.

An item is purchased for $200 and is sold for $350.

5. Find the dollar amount of the markon.

6. Find the markon percent based on cost.

7. Find the markon percent based on selling price.

An item is bought for $75. A markon of $40 is added.

8. Find the selling price.

9. Find the markon as a percent of cost.

10. Find the markon as a percent of selling price.

An item is purchased for $5 and is sold for $8.

11. Find the markon amount.

12. Find the markon as a percent of cost.

13. Find the markon as a percent of selling price.

An item receives a markon of $30, which is 60% of cost.

14. Find the cost.

15. Find the selling price.

16. Find the markon as a percent of selling price.

An item receives a markon of $32, which is 40% of the selling price.

17. Find the selling price.

18. Find the cost.

19. Find the markon as a percent of cost.

CHAPTER TEST

A rare book dealer purchases a set of first editions for $1,400. He applies 40% markon based on the cost price.

1. Find the markon amount.

2. Find the selling price.

A retailer, who owns several stores, places an order for 200 picture frames at $4.00 each. The transportation terms are F.O.B. Store. The discount terms are 2/10 E.O.M. The invoice is dated May 13. A markon of 75% of cost price is added per picture frame.

3. Who pays the transportation charges?

4. Who has title to the goods while they are being transported?

5. What is the last day for which the cash discount is allowed?

6. What amount of payment if the invoice is paid on June 2?

7. Find the total amount of markon, neglecting the discount.

8. Find the selling price of each picture frame.

9. Find the markon as a percent of the selling price.

The retail price of an item is $8.96. The markon as a percent of cost is 60%.

10. Find the retail price as a percent of cost.

11. Find the cost price.

12. Find the markon amount.

A computer is purchased by a retailer for $280 and is sold for $500.

13. Find the markon amount.

14. Find the markon percent based on cost.

15. Find the markon percent based on selling price.

16. An item receives a markon of 60% of cost. Find the markon as a percent of the selling price.

17. An item receives a markon of 50% of the selling price. Find the markon as a percent of cost.

An item receives a markon of $4.80, which is 80% of cost.

18. Find the cost.

19. Find the markon as a percent of selling price.

20. Find the selling price.

ANSWERS

5.1
1. $400
2. $1,200
3. $1.40
4. $2.24
5. $200
6. $280
7. The supplier
8. 1,200
9. $0.45
10. $0.27
11. $0.72
12. 240
13. The retailer
14. The retailer
15. March 25
16. $1,176
17. $4.90
18. $4.41
19. $9.31
20. $400
21. $680
22. 170%

5.2
1. $200
2. $100
3. 160%
4. $300
5. $180
6. $80
7. $36
8. 45%

5.3
1. $220
2. 40%
3. $1,860
4. 55%
5. $0.60
6. 67%
7. $445
8. $745
9. $300
10. $15
11. September 10
12. $2,940
13. The retailer
14. The supplier

15. $9
16. 60%

5.4   1. (a) 80%, (b) 44%
2. (a) 100%, (b) 50%
3. (a) 100%, (b) 50%
4. (a) 75%, (b) 43%
5. (a) 65%, (b) 39%
6. $30
7. $80
8. 38%
9. $216
10. $144
11. 150%
12. $6.80
13. $8.50
14. 20%
15. $560
16. 60%
17. 37.5%

5.5   1. 20%
2. 43%
3. 67%
4. 150%
5. $150
6. 75%
7. 43%
8. $115
9. 53%
10. 35%
11. $3
12. 60%
13. 38%
14. $50
15. $80
16. 38%
17. $80
18. $48
19. 67%

CHAPTER TEST

1. $560
2. $1,960
3. The supplier
4. The supplier
5. June 10
6. $784
7. $600
8. $7
9. 43%
10. 160%
11. $5.60
12. $3.36
13. $220
14. 79%
15. 44%
16. 38%
17. 100%
18. $6
19. 44%
20. $10.80

6 Average Markon

In Chapters 4 and 5 you worked with markon for individual items. Markon was based first on selling price and then on cost. In this chapter, unless otherwise stated, we will consider markon as a percent of selling price. But we will not work with individual items. Rather we will be interested in the markon for a number of items taken together.

After completing this chapter you will be able to:

- Calculate the average markon for several items.

- Interpret and use a spreadsheet showing cost, selling price, and markon for many items.

- Find the average markon for a number of large purchases.

- Use and explain the relationship of average markon to planned markon.

6.1 CALCULATING MARKON FOR TWO OR THREE ITEMS

A retail store or merchandise department stocks hundreds and, in some cases, thousands of different items. The cost prices vary, as do the retail selling prices.

Markon is a central factor in profits and stores must make a profit to stay in business. Stores and other businesses that sell goods and services plan their profits, and also plan the markon, by the month and by the quarter (three months). The retailer's main concern, therefore, is not with the markon for individual items but with the overall markon for all or most of the items in the store. A retailer will be happy to make only a small profit on some items if a large profit can be made on others.

If the cost of an individual item is $3.00 and the retail price is $5.00, then the markon amount is $2.00 and the markon percent based on the selling price is 40%.

Selling Price × Markon Percent = Markon Amount
Markon Percent = Markon Amount/Selling Price
Markon Percent = 2/5 = 0.40 = 40%

Item A is purchased for $3.00 and is sold at a price of $5.00; item B is purchased for $2.00 and is sold for $3.00. Table 6–1 shows a combined markon for the two items.

The average markon shown in Table 6–1 is found by dividing the total markon, $3.00, by the $8.00: 3/8 = 0.375 = 37.5%. You cannot find the markon percent by averaging the percents of different items. You must use the dollar amounts.

TABLE 6–1

Combined Markon

	Cost	+	Markon	=	Retail	% Markon
Item A	$3.00	+	$2.00	=	$5.00	40%
Item B	$2.00	+	$1.00	=	$3.00	33.3%
Total	$5.00	+	$3.00	=	$8.00	37.5%

Example 1:

A buyer purchased a comb for $1.00, a hair brush for $3.00, and a hand mirror for $4.00. The comb was retailed for $1.50, the hair brush for $4.50, and the hand mirror for $10.00. Find the average markon for all three items.

Solution:

Markon amounts are found by subtracting costs from retail prices. Markon percents are found by dividing total markon by total retail price, as shown in Table 6–2.

TABLE 6–2

Sample Markon Calculations

	Cost	+	Markon	=	Retail	Markon %
Comb	$1.00	+	$0.50	=	$ 1.50	
Brush	$3.00	+	$1.50	=	$ 4.50	
Mirror	$4.00	+	$6.00	=	$10.00	
Total	$8.00	+	$8.00	=	$16.00	50%

Example 2:

The following items are purchased for the cost prices shown. Markon as a percent of selling price is also shown: Iron supplement @ $1.45, markon 40%; vitamins @ $3.04, markon 20%.

    a. For each item find the selling price to the nearest cent.

    b. Find the average markon.

Solution:

    a. The following equation shows cost and markon percent based on selling price for the iron supplement:

$$\text{Cost Percent} + \text{Markon Percent} = \text{Selling Price Percent}$$
$$\text{Cost Percent} + 40\% = 100\%$$

Therefore, the cost as a percent of selling price is 60%. We can now use a percent equation.

$$\text{Selling Price} \times \text{Cost Percent} = \text{Cost}$$
$$\text{Selling Price} \times 60\% = 1.45$$

$$\text{Selling Price} = 1.45/0.60 \quad = 2.42$$
$$\text{Markon} \quad = 2.42 - 1.45 = 0.97$$

Similarly, for the vitamins:

$$\text{Selling Price} \quad = 3.04/0.80 \quad = 3.80$$
$$\text{Markon} \quad = 3.80 - 3.04 = 0.76$$

b.
$$\text{Total selling price} = 2.42 + 3.80 = 6.22$$
$$\text{Total markon} \quad = 0.97 + 0.76 = 1.73$$
$$\text{Average markon} = 1.73 \div 6.22 = 27.8\%$$

PRACTICE 6.1

1. A buyer purchases a necktie for $2.00 and a shirt for $4.00. He retails the necktie for $4.00 and the shirt for $5.00. Find the average markon percent for the two items.

2. A store owner purchases a table for $10.00, and a chair for $5.00. She retails the table for $20.00 and the chair for $10.00. Find the average markon percent based on selling price for the two items.

A buyer makes the following purchases:

    a. A pair of jeans: $20.00

    b. A blouse: $10.00

    c. A sweater: $30.00

The following retail prices were placed on the items:

    a. The pair of jeans: $30.00

    b. The blouse: $20.00

    c. The sweater: $55.00

3. Find the markon for each item.

4. For each item find the markon percent based on selling price.

5. Find the average markon percent.

The following items are purchased by a retailer. The cost and markon percent of selling price for each item are shown.

  a. Computer: cost $180, markon 10%

  b. Printer: cost $320, markon 20%

  c. Copier: cost $500, markon 50%

6. Find the selling price for each item.

7. Find the markon amount for each item.

8. Find the average markon percent for the three items.

6.2 AVERAGE MARKON FOR A LARGE NUMBER OF ITEMS

A retail store or merchandise department of a department store classifies goods according to categories. For example, a Bed and Bath store or department stocks sheets, pillow cases, bath towels, and similar items.

Retailers or department managers want to know which classes of items are contributing to profits, and what markon amounts or percents are most successful. These managers also want to know which products are not selling so that strategies can be changed. To accomplish these objectives, store owners must keep records that summarize sales information.

Retailers plan ahead by establishing markon percent for each class of goods and by finding the average for all of the classes in a store or department. This process begins with the assignment of planned markons, as shown in Table 6–3.

Retailers must keep track of actual markon compared with planned markon. This requires records of quantities of sales, not only individual items. The average of the planned markon percents in Table 6–3 is not the average of the given values because these are only a sample. Other items are not listed but are part of the department's inventory. Also, the

TABLE 6–3

Planned Markon Percentages

Class	Planned Markon %
Sheets	46%
Pillow Cases	45%
Mattress Covers	44%
Wash Cloths	44%
Bath Towels	48%
Bath Mats	47%
Kitchen Towels	45%
Average Markon	47%

planned markon percent is not the average of the markon percents but must be computed based on dollar amounts.

The spreadsheet is a powerful computer program that is used to maintain financial records in many areas of business. A spreadsheet is made up of rows and columns that intersect in cells. The cells are named by letters for columns and numbers for rows. For example the cell C6 is at the intersection of column C and row 6. The spreadsheet in Figure 6–1 shows the costs of items in stock and the retail value according to prices that have been set. Also shown are the markon percent and the planned markon percent.

PRACTICE 6.2

For each class of item listed in Table 6–4, page 88, find: the markon, the markon percent, the total markon, and the total markon percent. Use a spreadsheet program if one is available. If a spreadsheet program is not available, use a calculator to compute the different values.

	A	B	C	D	E	F
		Cost Value	Retail Value	Markon	Actual Markon %	Plan Markon %
1						
2	1. Sheets	10,000	20,000	10,000	50	46
3	2. Pillow Cases	8,000	12,000	4,000	33	45
4	3. Mattress Covers	5,000	8,000	3,000	38	44
5	4. Wash Cloths	3,000	6,000	3,000	50	44
6	5. Bath Towels	19,680	41,000	21,320	52	48
7	6. Bath Mats	2,000	5,000	3,000	60	47
8	7. Kitchen Towels	4,000	8,000	4,000	50	45
9	TOTAL	51,680	100,000	48,320		
10	ACTUAL AVERAGE MARKON				48	
11	PLAN AVERAGE MARKON					47

FIGURE 6–1
Bed and Bath Spreadsheet.

TABLE 6–4

Calculating Markon and Markon Percent

Class	Cost	Retail	Markon	Actual %	Plan %
Jeans	25,000	50,000	1. _____	2. _____	49
Blouses	12,000	20,000	3. _____	4. _____	44
Tops	5,000	8,000	5. _____	6. _____	42
Slacks	10,000	20,000	7. _____	8. _____	45
Sweaters	8,000	13,000	9. _____	10. _____	46
Jackets	10,000	13,000	11. _____	12. _____	46
Total	13. _____	14. _____	15. _____	16. _____	
Actual %					
Plan %					45

6.3 AVERAGE MARKON FOR SEVERAL COST PRICES AND ONE RETAIL PRICE

Retailers purchase items at various times, in different quantities, and sometimes from different vendors. The result of this activity is that a retailer routinely has a large number of one type of item purchased at different prices.

Example:

A buyer purchases 200 coats @ $100.00 from manufacturer *A*, 200 coats @ $75.00 from manufacturer *B*, and 100 coats @ $80.00 from manufacturer *C*. He plans to offer the 500 coats for one retail price of $150. If all the coats sell, what is the average markon percent?

Solution:

As in the previous section, the spreadsheet provides a handy method to solve this problem (see Figure 6–2).

	A	B	C	D	E	F	G	H
1	Vendor	Number	Cost Price	Total Cost	Selling Price	Total Sales	Markon	Markon %
2	A	200	100	20,000	150	30,000	10,000	33
3	B	200	75	15,000	150	30,000	15,000	50
4	C	100	80	8,000	150	15,000	7,000	47
5	Total	500		43,000		75,000	32,000	43

FIGURE 6–2
Spreadsheet
for Coats.

▌ PRACTICE 6.3

1. a. For each item listed in Figure 6–3, find: the total cost, the total sales amount, the markon amount, and markon percent. Then find the average markon percent.

   b. The following purchases are made for a Father's Day Sale:
      Manufacturer A: 400 sport shirts @ $5.00
      Manufacturer B: 300 sport shirts @ $4.00
      Manufacturer C: 300 sport shirts @ $4.50

   The shirts are to be advertised for $7.99 each. Set up a table or spreadsheet.

2. Find the average markon percent if all of the shirts are sold.

   c. A buyer is planning a children's dress sale for the spring season. The merchandise manager suggests that the total sale should result in a markon of 40% of the total sales. The buyer made the following purchases:
      Manufacturer A: 100 dresses @ $4.00
      Manufacturer B: 100 dresses @ $3.75
      Manufacturer C: 100 dresses @ $3.50

   The buyer plans to have one retail price for all the dresses. Determine the retail price in order to obtain a 40% average markon.

6.4 AVERAGE MARKON FOR ONE COST PRICE AND SEVERAL RETAIL PRICES

Retailers frequently have sales during which items are sold at reduced prices. These sales take place frequently in January and sometimes for special events. In addition, retailers and department stores also reduce prices when they are overstocked or have carried an item for a long time. Even during a sale that lasts several days, prices are sometimes lowered in order to sell goods as quickly as possible. It is, therefore, common for a retailer to sell similar items for different prices.

	A	B	C	D	E	F	G	H
1	Vendor	Number	Cost Price	Total Cost	Selling Price	Total Sales	Markon	Markon %
2	A	100	10		19.99			
3	B	50	12		19.99			
4	C	50	15		19.99			
5	Total	200						

FIGURE 6-3

Answer spreadsheet for Practice 6.3, Problem 1a.

To determine markon and average markon for items sold at different prices, use a method similar to that used for different cost prices. Once again, the spreadsheet, or a table similar to a computer spreadsheet, offers a useful method for computing.

At the end of a particular selling season, manufacturers are sometimes left with a group of items in various styles, colors, sizes, and prices. Such a group of items is referred to as a job lot or lot. A buyer interested in purchasing the entire lot for a sale must examine the items to determine the retail prices that should be established for the sale.

Example:

A buyer is offered a lot of 500 coats. She determines that 200 coats can be priced at $99.00, 200 can be priced at $89.00, and the remainder can be priced at $79.00. What is the most the buyer can afford to pay for the lot if she wishes to achieve a 40% markon?

Solution:

Total retail sales are:

$$200 \times 99 = 19,800$$
$$200 \times 89 = 17,800$$
$$200 \times 70 = 7,900$$
$$\text{Total} = 45,500$$

To find the cost the buyer can afford, begin with the equation stating the relationship between cost and markon as percents of sales. Since the markon is to be 40%, then:

$$\text{Cost Percent} + \text{Markon Percent} = 100\%$$
$$60\% + 40\% = 100\%$$

We can now find the total to be spent on the lot

$$45,500 \times 0.60 = 27,300$$

The buyer can afford to spend $27,300 for the coats.

PRACTICE 6.4

A buyer is offered a lot of 300 ladies umbrellas. She determines that 150 umbrellas should be priced at $10.00, 100 umbrellas at $8.00, and the remainder at $7.00. An average markon of 42% is planned for the entire lot.

1. Find the total selling price of the lot.

2. Find the most that the buyer can pay for the lot and achieve the desired markon.

A buyer is considering the purchase of a job lot for an end-of-month sale. After examining the lot of ladies gloves, she has determined that:

150 can be priced at $9.00

200 can be priced at $8.00

150 can be priced at $7.00

She plans an average markon of 43%.

3. What is the total selling price of the goods?

4. What total cost price can be paid to achieve the desired markon?

A buyer purchases a lot consisting of:

100 men's suits to be retailed at $79.95

100 men's suits to be retailed at $89.95

5. Find the cost price if the average markon is 36%.

6.5   PROPORTIONAL SALES TO ACHIEVE A PLANNED MARKON PERCENT (OPTIONAL)

Occasionally a buyer may be able to purchase merchandise consisting of different fabrics, different colors, and different styles. Some items will have greater consumer appeal than others. As a result, the buyer plans to establish different retail prices even though he pays the same cost price for all of the items.

The buyer's problem is to determine how many of the total units to price at each of the established retail prices to obtain the desired average markon percent.

Example:

A buyer purchases 200 ladies wallets at $1.50 each. He plans to establish two retail prices of $2.39 and $3.89. The planned markon is 40%. How many of the wallets should he sell at each price?

Solution:

The total cost is 200 × $1.50 = $300. Next, the total desired amount of sales should be determined. Since the markon is 40% of the sales, the total cost price is 60%. We have:

$$60\% \times \text{Sales} = \$300$$
$$\text{Sales} = 300/0.60 = 500$$
$$\text{Total sales amount is } \$500$$

Since a total of 200 wallets are to be sold, the quantity x can be considered the amount sold at $2.39 and the quantity $(200 - x)$ can be considered the amount sold at $2.89. The total sales must equal $500; thus the equation:

$$2.39x + 2.89 (200 - x) = 500$$
$$2.39x + 578 - 2.89x = 500$$
$$-0.50x = -78$$
$$x = 156$$
$$200 - x = 44$$

156 wallets are sold at $2.39; 44 wallets are sold at $2.89.

PRACTICE 6.5

1. Prove that the quantities found in the previous example yield the desired amount of sales.

A buyer purchases a group of 120 skirts at $6.00 each. The plan is to establish retail prices of $9.00 and $12.00 with an average markon of 40%.

2.. Find the total planned sales amount.

3. Find the number to be sold at each price in order to achieve the planned markon.

A buyer purchases 150 hats at $10.00 each. She wants to achieve a markon percent of 50%. After examining the merchandise, she plans to retail some of the hats for $19, and the remainder for $22.

4. Find the number to be sold at each price in order to achieve the planned markon.

5. A buyer purchases 100 tennis racquets at $12.00 each. He plans to retail some at $19.00 and the remainder at $25.00 and he plans to achieve an average planned markon of 45%. Find the number to be sold at each price in order to achieve the planned markon.

VOCABULARY REVIEW

Average Markon: The average of several markon amounts.

Average Markon Percent: The average percent based on different markon amounts. The average percent is computed by using dollar amounts, not by taking the average of different percents.

Spreadsheet: A computer program that arranges information (usually numbers) in rows and columns. The rows and columns intersect in cells that are identified by the letter of the column and number of the row, for example, D4. Spreadsheets are a useful tool in presenting and analyzing financial data.

CHAPTER TEST

A buyer makes the following purchases:

a. A shirt: $12.00

b. A jacket: $25.00

c. A sweater: $18.00

The following retail prices were placed on the items:

a. The shirt: $24.00

b. The jacket: $40.00

c. The sweater: $30.00

1. Find the markon for each item.

2. For each item find the markon percent based on selling price.

3. Find the average markon percent.

For each class of items listed in Table 6–5, find: the markon, the markon percent, the total markon, and the total markon percent. Use a spreadsheet program if one is available. If a spreadsheet program is not available, use a calculator to compute the different values.

A buyer is considering the purchase of a job lot for a sale. After examining the lot of ladies shoes she has determined that:

100 can be priced at $29.00

200 can be priced at $39.00

150 can be priced at $79.00

She plans an average markon of 40%.

9. What is the total selling price of the goods?

10. What total cost price can be paid to achieve the desired markon?

TABLE 6–5

Calculating Markon and Markon Percent

Class	Cost	Retail	Markon	Actual %	Plan %
Jeans	20,000	40,000	20,000	4. _____	49
T-shirts	9,000	20,000	5. _____	6. _____	44
Hats	6,000	10,000	7. _____	8. _____	42

ANSWERS

6.1
1. 33%
2. 50%
3. (a) $10, (b) $10, (c) $25
4. (a) 33%, (b) 50%, (c) 45%
5. 43%
6. (a) $200, (b) $400, (c) $1,000
7. (a) $20, (b) $80, (c) $500
8. 38%

6.2
1. $25,000
2. 50%
3. $8,000
4. 40%
5. $3,000
6. 38%
7. $10,000
8. 50%
9. $5,000
10. 38%
11. $3,000
12. 23%
13. $70,000
14. $124,000
15. $54,000
16. 44%

6.3
1. See Figure 6–4
2. 43%
3. $6.25

6.4
1. $2,650
2. $1,537
3. $4,000
4. $2,280
5. $10,873.60

6.5
1. $372.84 + $127.16 = $500
2. $1,200
3. 80 @ $9.00, 40 @ $12.00
4. 100 @ $19.00, 50 @ $22.00
5. 53 @ $19.00, 47 @ $25.00

CHAPTER TEST

1. (a) $12, (b) $15, (c) $12

2. (a) 50%, (b) 38%, (c) 40%

	A	B	C	D	E	F	G	H
1	Vendor	Number	Cost Price	Total Cost	Selling Price	Total Sales	Markon	Markon
2	A	100	10	1,000	19.99	1,999	999	50%
3	B	50	12	600	19.99	999.5	399.5	40%
4	C	50	15	750	19.99	999.5	249.5	25%
5	Total	200		2,350		3,998	1,648	41%

FIGURE 6–4

Answer spreadsheet for Practice 6.3, Problem 1a.

3. 41%

4. 50%

5. 11,000

6. 55%

7. $4,000

8. 40%

9. $22,550

10. $13,530

7 The Buyer's Purchase Order

A purchase order is a form that is recognized as giving the buyer authorization from the store or company to buy items or goods. Most vendors will not fill an order unless it is made using a purchase order. Purchase orders are numbered and thus provide an easy method for tracking an order. Purchase orders are also formatted so that buyer and vendor can easily find all the necessary information.

After completing this chapter you will be able to:

- Describe all necessary elements of a purchase order.

- Recognize different kinds of purchase orders.

- Use correct mathematical procedures to complete the buyer's purchase order.

7.1 KINDS OF PURCHASE ORDERS AND QUANTITIES

There are many different kinds of purchase orders and it is useful to know their names and uses. The following are some of the types and uses of purchase orders:

A *regular order* is written for new items.

A *reorder,* also referred to as a fill-in order, is used to buy an additional quantity of new items.

A *standing order* is an arrangement authorizing a supplier to ship a specified quantity at stated times, such as at the beginning of each month.

A *special order* is an order for an item not regularly stocked by a store. Generally this is done as a service for a particular customer.

A *blanket order* is an order placed in advance for an entire season. The buyer periodically draws a quantity from the order.

An order *on memo* or a *consignment order* means that the buyer takes goods with the agreement that the retailer will pay for the goods after sales have been made and he or she will return the unsold portion of the order.

A *back order* covers items on an original order that cannot be filled by the manufacturer at the time of the regular order.

In order to complete a purchase order, the buyer must know the supplier's prices. Suppliers use a number of different ways to quote prices, most of which depend on quantities. The following are some of the more commonly used forms of pricing:

Single item and the unit cost: The price quoted is for one item. For example, one dress costs $32.75. The unit cost is listed as $32.75.

Dozen and the unit cost: The price quote is for one dozen items. For example, the price of 12 bottles of shampoo is $14.00. The unit cost is $14.00 since one dozen is a unit.

Gross and the unit cost: The price quoted is for 144 items (or 12 dozen). For example, the price of the 144 items may be $72.00. The unit cost is $72.00 since one gross is a unit.

Bag or sack and the unit cost: The price quoted is for the contents of a prepared bag or sack. For example, a sack of potatoes may weigh 50 pounds and may cost $10.00. The unit cost is $10.00 since the sack is a unit.

Yard or bolt and the unit cost: Cloth is generally sold by the yard, in which case it (the yard) is the unit. A bolt is a long piece of rolled fabric. The exact length of a bolt may vary, but a supplier and buyer will know the size of the bolt in a given transaction.

Example:

Women's belts are quoted by the supplier at $42.50 per dozen. Find the cost of purchasing 10 dozen.

Solution:

The unit is one dozen, therefore the cost price is:

$$10 \times 42.50 = 425$$

The total cost price is $425.00.

PRACTICE 7.1

Complete the partial purchase order shown in Figure 7–1 by filling in the total costs.

Quantity Purchase	Unit Cost	Total Cost
100 blouses	12.75 ea.	1.
12 dozen belts	37.50 a doz	2.
8 gross pencils	4.00 a gross	3.
36 prepack key chains	6.75 a prepack	4.
20 bags fertilizer	4.50 per bag	5.
86 yards velvet	16.50 per yd	6.
3 bolts muslin	32.00 per bolt	7.
11 barrels nails	8.00 per barrel	8.
	Total	9.

FIGURE 7–1
Partial purchase order.

A retailer orders 25 dozen T-shirts at $39.00 a dozen. Transportation terms are F.O.B. Factory. Cash discount terms are 2/10/N30. The invoice is dated April 24.

10. Find the cost of the T-shirts.

11. Who has title to the goods during transportation?

12. Who pays for transportation?

13. What is the last date on which the discount can be taken?

14. What is the amount of the cash discount?

15. What amount must be paid if the invoice payment is made on May 4?

A retailer orders 45 yards of fabric at $12.85 a yard. Transportation terms are F.O.B. Store. Cash discount terms are 3/10/2/20/N30. The invoice is dated May 15.

16. Find the cost of the fabric.

17. Who has title to the goods during transportation?

18. Who pays for transportation?

19. What is the last date on which a discount can be taken?

20. What amount must be paid if the invoice payment is made on May 24?

21. What amount must be paid on June 14?

7.2 THE PURCHASE ORDER: COST PRICE, SELLING PRICE, AND MARKON

In order for a retail store or department to achieve profits as planned, it is important that a buyer prepare selling prices at the same time that items are ordered. Selling prices are written on the store's copy of a purchase order and also on the supplier's copy if the supplier is to preticket the goods, that is, if the supplier is to include price tags on the items.

Style Number	Quantity	Unit Cost	Total Cost	Unit Retail	Total Retail	Markon %
676	24	10.00	1. _____	20.00	2. _____	3. _____
712	12	8.00	4. _____	12.00	5. _____	6. _____
1,101	12	12.00	7. _____	20.00	8. _____	9. _____

FIGURE 7-2
Partial purchase order.

Buyers regularly write several items on a purchase order. Each item may have its own markon and markon percent. The markon percent to be obtained from the total of several items is the purchase markon percent for that order.

The methods used to compute prices and markon percents are the same as those used in previous chapters.

PRACTICE 7.2

A buyer purchases quantities of ladies blouses. They are different styles and have different cost prices and retail prices. Complete the partial purchase order shown in Figure 7–2, which shows unit costs, total costs, unit retail prices, total retail amounts, and markon percent.

10. Find the total cost of the items listed.

11. Find the total selling price of the items listed.

12. Find the purchase markon percent for the entire order.

Style Number	Quantity	Unit Cost	Total Cost	Unit Retail	Total Retail	Markon %
717	36	6.00	13. _____	9.95	14. _____	15. _____
832	400	11.75	16. _____	19.95	17. _____	18. _____
1,122	650	14.95	19. _____	24.00	20. _____	21. _____
401	24	11.25	22. _____	21.00	23. _____	24. _____

Figure 7–3
Partial purchase order.

Complete the partial purchase order shown in Figure 7–3.

25. Find the total cost of the items listed.

26. Find the total selling price of the items listed.

27. Find the purchase markon percent for the entire order.

28. The cash discount terms are 2/10–X60 and the invoice is dated December 3. What is the last day for payment to obtain the cash discount?

ANSWERS

7.1
1. $1,275
2. $450
3. $32
4. $243
5. $90
6. $1,419
7. $96
8. $88
9. $3,693
10. $975
11. The retailer
12. The retailer
13. May 4
14. $19.50
15. $955.50
16. $578.25
17. The supplier
18. The supplier
19. June 4
20. $560.90
21. $578.25

7.2
1. $240
2. $480
3. 50%
4. $96
5. $144
6. 33%
7. $144
8. $240
9. 40%
10. $480
11. $864
12. 44%
13. $216
14. $358.20
15. 40%
16. $4,700
17. $7,980
18. 41%
19. $9,717.50
20. $15,600
21. 38%
22. $270
23. $504

24. 46%
25. $14,903.50
26. $24,442.20
27. 39%
28. February 11

Part II Computing and Covering Expenses

8 Gross Margin

In Part I of this text you learned the concepts and skills required to do the calculations used in purchasing goods and establishing prices. In Part II you will learn about the various expenses that must be considered by the retailer. These expenses directly affect the retailer as he or she prepares to set prices that will cover expenses, yield a reasonable profit, and permit competition with other stores.

No store or business can long operate if it does not sell its goods at prices high enough to pay for the goods purchased and to pay its expenses. In this chapter you will learn more about the costs that are directly connected with the purchase of items to sell.

After completing this chapter you will be able to:

- Explain gross margin.

- Explain ways to increase gross margin.

- Explain how stock turnover can increase gross margin.

- Solve practical problems about gross margin.

8.1 COST OF GOODS SOLD

Stores and businesses consider expenses in levels or layers. The first level contains those expenses that are directly related to the item sold. These costs include the cost price of the item, transportation charges, cash discounts, adjustments from the vendor, and the alteration and workroom costs needed to prepare merchandise for sale. The total of these costs and deductions is called the cost of goods sold.

Gross margin, also called gross profit, is the amount remaining after the cost of goods sold has been deducted from the total sales for a particular product or a given quantity of inventory. Gross margin percent is an important figure in retailing because it is an indication of how profitable a product or an entire business is likely to be.

The **cost of goods sold** is calculated by adding:

Total cost price for the product after cash discounts

Transportation charges

Alteration costs and workroom costs

and then subtracting from this total:

Vendor returns, that is, items returned because of damage or incorrect orders.

Example 1:

An order for 22 computers is purchased at a cost price of $8,600.00. A 3% cash discount is given. Workroom costs to prepare the computers for sale amount to $190.00. All of the computers are sold for $13,970.00.

Find (a) the cost of goods sold, (b) the gross margin, and (c) the gross margin percent.

Solution:

a. Cost Price: 8,600
      Less cash discount   −258   (8,600 × 3%)
      Cost price after discount   8,342
      Plus workroom costs   +190
      Cost of Goods Sold   8,532

b. Gross Margin: 13,970 − 8,532 = 5,438

c. Gross Margin Percent: 5,438 ÷ 13,970 = 0.389 = 39%

Example 2:

An order of 5,000 shirts costs $20,000.00. The transportation terms are F.O.B. Factory. The transportation charges are $425.00. The cash discount terms are 3/10/2/20/N30. The invoice is dated March 3 and the bill is paid on March 13. Workroom costs to prepare the merchandise for sale amount to $390.00. An allowance of $1,200.00 is made for 600 imperfect shirts. The good shirts are all sold for $8.00 each. The imperfect shirts are sold for $4.00 each.

For the entire inventory of 5,000 shirts, find (a) the cost of goods sold, (b) the gross margin amount, and (c) the gross margin percent.

Solution:

a. Total Cost Price	20,000	
Less cash discount	−600	
	19,400	
Plus transportation charges	+425	
	19,825	
Plus workroom costs	+390	
	20,215	
Less vendor's allowance	1,200	
Cost of Goods Sold	19,015	
b. Perfect shirts	35,200	(4,400 × 8)
Imperfect shirts	2,400	(600 × 4)
Total Sales	37,600	
Less Cost of Goods Sold	19,015	
Gross Margin	18,585	

c. Gross Margin Percent: $18,585 \div 37,600 = 0.494 = 49.4\%$

PRACTICE 8.1

An order for 150 pairs of shoes is purchased at a cost price of $25 for each pair. A 2% cash discount is given. Costs to prepare the merchandise for sale amount to $85.00. All of the shoes are sold for $6,250.00.

1. Find the total cost price before discount.

2. Find the amount of the cash discount.

3. Find the cost of goods sold.

4. Find the gross margin.

5. Find the gross margin percent.

An order of 4,000 sweaters costs $18,000.00. The transportation terms are F.O.B. Factory. The transportation charges are $325.00. The cash discount terms are 2/10/N30. The invoice is dated August 23 and the bill is paid on September 2. Workroom costs to prepare the merchandise for sale amounts to $185.00. An allowance of $700.00 is made for 350 imperfect sweaters. The good shirts are all sold for $7.00 each. The imperfect shirts are sold for $3.50 each.

6. Find the cost price for an individual sweater.

7. Find the total cost price after taking the cash discount.

8. Find the cost of goods sold.

9. Find the total selling price of the sweaters.

10. Find the gross margin.

11. Find the gross margin percent.

A buyer places an order for 200 dozen boxes of juice at $4.20 a dozen. The goods are delivered F.O.B. Store. Preparation for sale costs $48.00. An allowance of $8.40 is made for 2 dozen bottles lost in transit. The juice is sold for $0.60 a box.

12. Find the cost of goods sold.

13. Find the total sales amount.

14. Find the gross margin.

15. Find the gross margin percent.

8.2 USING GROSS MARGIN IN PLANNING

Gross margin is important not only in keeping records of sales but also in planning ahead. Managers of large department stores as well as owners of small retail stores set targets for amounts of sales and for expenses. They attempt to determine in advance what they will be earning and whether they will be able to pay their bills. In this planning process, the gross margin percent is an important indicator.

The term commonly used for total sales dollars after any discounts is *net sales.*

In financial reports and news items about finances, you will often see amounts such as $1.5 million. This is a way of writing $1,500,000. For most people $1.5 million is easier to understand.

Example 1:

A company's net sales are $1.7 million. Gross margin is 40%. Find the dollar amount of the gross margin.

Solution:

$$\$1.7 \text{ million} = \$1,700,000$$
$$\$1,700,000 \times 40\% = \$680,000$$

Example 2:

A store's six-month plan projects net sales to be $222,000.00. The planned gross margin is 35.2%. Find the dollar amount of the gross margin.

Solution:

$$0.352 \times 222,000 = 78,144$$

The six-month planned gross margin is $78,144.00.

PRACTICE 8.2

Find the gross margin as a percent of net sales for each of the following.

1. Gross Margin: $35,000; Net Sales: $90,000.

2. Gross Margin: $3,000; Net Sales: $11,000.

3. Gross Margin: $1,100,000; Net Sales: $3,905,000.

4. Gross Margin: $1.5 million; Net Sales: $5.4 million.

A retailer has projected net sales of $250,000 and a projected gross margin of 39.5%.

5. Find the gross margin dollar amount.

6. Find the cost of goods sold.

A retailer has projected net sales of $1.2 million and a projected gross margin of 43.2%.

7. Find the gross margin dollar amount.

8. Find the cost of goods sold.

A retailer has projected net sales of $1.9 million and projected cost of goods sold of $1.25 million.

9. Find the dollar amount of the gross margin.

10. Find the gross margin percent.

ANSWERS

8.1
1. $3,750
2. $75
3. $3,760
4. $2,490
5. 39.8%
6. $4.50
7. $17,640
8. $17,450
9. $26,775
10. $9,325
11. 34.8%
12. $879.60
13. $1,425.60
14. $546
15. 38.3%

8.2
1. 38.9%
2. 27.3%
3. 28.2%
4. 27.8%
5. $98,750
6. $151,250
7. $518,400
8. $681,600
9. $650,000
10. 34.2%

9 Expenses

In Chapter 8 you learned about the first level of costs that a retail business must consider. The largest amount in the first level is the cost price of merchandise to be sold. There are some smaller costs resulting from alterations and transportation that may be added to this basic cost and there are possible discount deductions that are subtracted from this cost. The result, with these adjustments, is called the *cost-of-goods sold*. Gross margin is the amount remaining when the cost-of-goods sold is subtracted from net sales.

In this chapter you will learn about the next level of costs that a retailer must consider. These are the general expenses that businesses incur. They include things such as salaries, rent, utilities, advertising, and insurance payments.

After completing this chapter you will be able to:

- Explain the different retail expenses.

- Calculate different expense amounts as percents of net sales.

- Prorate expenses according to the amounts of departmental sales.

9.1 EXPENSE CATEGORIES

The following are the major categories needed to classify the expenses of a retail business.

Payroll: Almost all retail businesses have employees working for them. A small business may employ only a few salespersons. Larger stores have buyers, delivery drivers, maintenance people, and possibly many others. All of these people must be paid. The salaries, hourly wages, commissions, bonuses, and prizes for contests all belong in the payroll category of expenses.

Property rental: Most businesses rent their stores and other facilities and must pay for their use.

Advertising: To increase sales, retail businesses present their products in newspapers, on radio and television, and through direct mail.

Taxes: There are different federal, state, and city business taxes levied on a business's sales and assets, such as property and inventory taxes. There are also employee-related taxes that a business must pay, such as unemployment, disability, and social security (FICA).

Supplies: In order to function efficiently, every business needs supplies, such as stationery, wrapping paper, and cleaning materials.

Nonprofessional services purchased: It has become common for businesses to purchase services according to need rather than to hire full-time employees. Even large companies often contract with outside agencies that perform services, such as delivery, repairs, or maintenance.

Travel: Retail businesses sometimes send employees, such as managers and buyers, to conventions or meetings to keep them informed about new product development and new business strategies. The expenses for these trips are listed as employee travel expenses.

Communications: This category includes postage, telephone, fax, electronic mail, and computer networking.

Pensions: Companies incur two general categories of pension expenses: payments to retired employees and contributions to pension funds.

Insurance: Businesses must protect themselves against unexpected events that may have serious economic consequences. A fire or flood could destroy inventory. An accident caused by a company employee or product sold could result in a lawsuit. Large and small businesses therefore carry insurance and must make premium payments to maintain these policies.

Professional services: Businesses periodically require the service of accountants, lawyers, and consultants. Small- and medium-sized companies hire people providing these services according to need.

Bad debts: Every business sometimes finds itself unable to collect money owed to it either from customers or from other businesses. Such bad debts represent money spent and anticipated sales dollars. These debts must therefore be categorized as an expense and subtracted from sales along with other expenses.

As part of the planning process, both large and small businesses, as well as departments within businesses, plan their expense categories both in dollar amounts and as percentages of sales.

Example:

The Sporting Goods Department of the Globe Department Store lists the following quarterly expenses:

Payroll	$10,000
Advertising	6,000
Supplies	3,000
Communications	1,000
Pensions	5,000
Insurance	4,000
Bad Debts	1,000

Net sales for the department are $100,000.00. Find each category as a percent of net sales.

Solution:

The percent for each category is found by dividing the expense amount by 100,000.00. The decimal is then converted to a percent. The percents are as follows:

Payroll	10%
Advertising	6%
Supplies	3%
Communications	1%
Pensions	5%
Insurance	4%
Bad Debts	1%

PRACTICE 9.1

The projected net sales for the dress department at the Globe Department Store are $200,000.00. The projected expenses are:

Payroll	$20,000
Insurance premiums	5,000
Equipment costs	2,000
Bad debts	3,000
Professional services	2,000
Communications	2,500
Supplies	1,500
Advertising	3,500

Find each of the following percent categories as a percent of projected net sales.

1. Payroll

2. Insurance premiums

3. Equipment costs

4. Bad debts

5. Professional services

6. Communications

7. Supplies

8. Advertising

The actual net sales for the Dress Department were $180,300. The actual expenses, rounded to the nearest hundred, were:

Payroll	$19,600
Insurance premiums	4,900
Equipment costs	1,100
Bad debts	2,700
Professional services	2,400
Communications	2,100
Supplies	900
Advertising	3,600

Find each of the following percent categories as a percent of projected net sales. Round each answer to the nearest tenth of a percent.

9. Payroll

10. Insurance premiums

11. Equipment costs

12. Bad debts

13. Professional services

14. Communications

15. Supplies

16. Advertising

9.2 ESTABLISHING SALES GOALS

When an individual makes plans to open a small retail store or when a large company establishes a new sales department, it is necessary for sales goals to be established so that the store or department can cover its expenses.

For example, if a store owner knows that the store's operating expenses come to $10,000.00 and that these expenses should be about 20% of net sales, then the store can calculate the sales needed.

Expense Percent × Net Sales = Expense Dollars
20% × Net Sales = 10,000

Since the net sales amount is multiplied by 20% (or 0.2), net sales can be obtained by itself by dividing each side of the equation by 20% or 0.2. This will yield:

$$\text{Net Sales} = 10,000 \div 0.2 = 50,000$$

Therefore, the sales amount needed to cover the anticipated expenses is $50,000.00.

PRACTICE 9.2

For each of the following examples find the net sales dollars needed to support the given expenses at the given percent rate. Round answers to the nearest thousand dollars.

Expense Amount	Expense Rate
1. $9,000	15%
2. $25,000	12.5%
3. $44,000	11%
4. $125,000	9%
5. $14,000	10.5%

9.3 PRORATING EXPENSES

People who operate businesses like to keep track of the profitability of different departments within a large store. If a department is profitable, the store managers may want to enlarge it to earn more profits. If a department is not profitable, the store managers will have to make a decision about whether to shrink the department to cut losses or possibly to invest in the department to correct mistakes and change direction.

A question arises about how to allocate or distribute expenses that belong to the entire store or company. A method often used is to prorate the expense among the different departments according to the percentage of sales for each department.

Example:

The management of the Globe Department Store has decided on major renovation of one floor. The cost is $250,000. The expense is to be prorated among the following departments based on net sales. The department and sales are as follows:

Department	Net Sales
Dresses	$400,000
Coats	200,000
Furs	100,000
Suits	175,000
Accessories	125,000

Find (a) the percent allocated to each department and (b) the amount to be paid by each department.

Solution:

a. Adding the sales figures, it is evident that total sales are $1,000,000. The percent allocated to each department is determined by dividing each sales amount by 1,000,000.

$$400,000 \div 1,000,000 = 0.40 = 40\%$$

Department	Net Sales	Percent
Dresses	$400,000	40%
Coats	200,000	20%
Furs	100,000	10%
Suits	175,000	17.5%
Accessories	125,000	12.5%
Total	$1,000,000	100%

b. To find the amount that must be paid by each department, we multiply the $250,000 amount by the prorated percent.

Department		
Dresses	250,000 × 0.40	= 100,000
Coats	250,000 × 0.20	= 50,000
Furs	250,000 × 0.10	= 25,000
Suits	250,000 × 0.175	= 43,750
Accessories	250,000 × 0.125	= 31,250
Total		= 250,000

PRACTICE 9.3

The managers of the Globe Department Store have decided to replace the canopy around the store. The expense will be $90,000. The expense will be prorated among the following selling departments according to sales.

Department	Sales
Handbags	$ 50,000
Gloves	25,000
Cosmetics	125,000
Stationery	100,000
Scarves	15,000
Umbrellas	35,000

Find, to the nearest tenth of a percent, the percent allocated to each department.

Department	Percent
Handbags	1. _____
Gloves	2. _____
Cosmetics	3. _____

Stationery	4. _____
Scarves	5. _____
Umbrellas	6. _____

Use the percent to find the amount, to the nearest dollar, that each department will pay.

Department	Amount
Handbags	7. _____
Gloves	8. _____
Cosmetics	9. _____
Stationery	10. _____
Scarves	11. _____
Umbrellas	12. _____

The management has decided to install six new point-of-sale cash registers (P.O.S. terminals) on the street floor. The total cost of the terminals and installation is $80,000. The departments on the street floor are to be charged for the expense. In this case the expense will be prorated based on the number of transactions, not on sales. The number of transactions for the previous year are as follows:

Department	Transactions
Men's furnishings	100,000
Men's shoes	10,000
Cosmetics	250,000
Costume jewelry	140,000

Find the percentage allocated to each department.

Department	Percent
Men's furnishings	13. _____

Men's shoes   14. _____

Cosmetics   15. _____

Costume
  jewelry   16. _____

Find the amount to be paid by each department.

Department   Amount

Men's fur-
  nishings   17. _____

Men's shoes   18. _____

Cosmetics   19. _____

Costume
  jewelry   20. _____

CHAPTER TEST

Explain the meaning of each of the following payroll categories.

1. Payroll

2. Pensions

3. Nonprofessional services purchased

4. Travel

5. Bad debts

The Sporting Goods Department of the Globe Department Store lists the following quarterly expenses:

Payroll	$15,600
Rent	6,700
Advertising	4,200
Supplies	1,600
Insurance	2,000

Net sales for the department are $125,000. Find each category as a percent of net sales.

Payroll	6. _____
Rent	7. _____
Advertising	8. _____
Supplies	9. _____
Insurance	10. _____

For each of the following find the net sales dollars needed to support the given expenses at the given percent rate. Round answers to the nearest hundred dollars.

	Expense Amount	Expense Rate
11.	$ 12,000	10%
12.	$ 21,000	9%
13.	$ 52,000	12.5%
14.	$180,000	15%
15.	$200,000	10.5%

The managers of the Globe Department Store have decided to renovate the third floor. The expense will be $60,000.00. The expense will be prorated among the following selling departments according to sales.

Department	Sales
Sportswear	$140,000
Yard furniture	35,000
Sports equipment	50,000
Music	80,000
TV	45,000

Find the percentage allocated to each department.

Department	Percent
Sportswear	16. _____
Yard furniture	17. _____
Sports equipment	18. _____
Music	19. _____
TV	20. _____

ANSWERS

9.1
1. 10%
2. 2.5%
3. 1%
4. 1.5%
5. 1%
6. 1.25%
7. 0.75%
8. 1.75%
9. 10.9%
10. 2.7%
11. 0.6%
12. 1.5%
13. 1.3%
14. 1.2%
15. 0.5%
16. 2%

9.2
1. $60,000
2. $200,000
3. $400,000
4. $1,389,000
5. $133,000

9.3
1. 14.3%
2. 7.1%
3. 35.7%
4. 28.6%
5. 4.3%
6. 10%
7. $12,870
8. $6,390
9. $32,130
10. $25,740
11. $3,870
12. $9,000
13. 20%
14. 2%
15. 50%
16. 28%
17. $16,000
18. $1,600
19. $40,000
20. $22,400

CHAPTER TEST

1. *Payroll* is amounts paid to workers; these amounts could be through hourly wages, weekly salaries, or other arrangements.

2. *Pension* includes amounts paid into a pension fund or paid out to retired workers.

3. *Nonprofessional services* is amount paid for services such as cleaning, maintenance, and delivery.

4. *Travel* is the cost of business travel by employees.

5. *Bad debts* are the amounts owed to a company for goods sold or services rendered, but not paid.

6. 12.5%

7. 5.4%

8. 3.4%

9. 1.3%

10. 1.6%

11. $120,000

12. $233,300

13. $416,000

14. $1,200,000

15. $1,904,800

16. 40%

17. 10%

18. 14.3%

19. 22.9%

20. 12.9%

10 Initial Markon

Previous chapters have explained markon and how individual markon and average markon percents are computed. This chapter describes how the markon percent is determined and what some of the ingredients are that help retailers establish a selling price.

After completing this chapter you will be able to:

- Explain the elements of the initial markon, often called markup.

- Calculate a markon and selling price based on given factors.

- Analyze merchandising situations related to initial markon.

10.1 ESTABLISHING THE INITIAL MARKON

The buyer, working with his or her manager, must consider a variety of factors when determining markon. These factors include shipping costs, expenses of running the store, and possible future markdowns in which prices are reduced. We can list the following conditions to be met for markon and selling price.

1. The selling price must cover operating expenses, freight expense, reductions in price, and reductions such as markdowns or employee discounts.

2. The price must allow the retailer to be competitive with other retailers.

3. The price should promote customer acceptance of the retailer's merchandise.

4. The price should result in increased sales and in satisfactory turnover of inventory.

5. The price should result in a satisfactory profit.

The following is a sample of how the elements of a markup (initial markon) might appear as percents of selling price or as parts of a dollar.

Expenses	22%	0.22
Reductions:		
Markdowns	7%	0.07
Stock shortages	1%	0.01
Employee discounts	2%	0.02
Alteration Costs	2%	0.02
Profit	10%	0.10
Total	44%	0.44

The total markon required is, therefore, 44%. If the retail price does not provide a 44% markon, the retailer will not meet all the markon needs.

Most expense categories, such as salaries, rent, utilities, and insurance, are either fixed or predictable. Alteration costs include services that are required in certain businesses, but for which no extra charges are made. Clothes are generally altered free of charge. Home appliances are installed at no additional cost. But there are additional costs because the people performing the alterations or installing the appliances must be paid. The costs are included in the selling prices of the clothes or appliances.

Reductions in price because of markdowns, stock shortages, and employee discounts can vary. These reductions do not represent money received as sales revenue, nor do they represent expenses paid. Rather these reductions represent a lack of revenue. It is necessary to take these reductions into account when establishing initial markon because if total sales do not reach the level planned, the retailer may not be able to pay expenses or will not earn desired profits.

Example:

An item costs the store $13.50. An initial markon of 44% is to be added. What selling price should be attached to the item?

Solution:

The markon accounts for 44% of the selling price. This means that the original cost accounts for 100% − 44%, or 56% of the selling price.

> That is: 56% × Selling Price = Cost Price
> Therefore: Selling Price = Cost Price ÷ 56%
>   = 13.50 ÷ 0.56
>   = 24.11

A price of $24.11 should be attached to the item.

PRACTICE 10.1

A retailer establishes the following table of markdown categories. She uses this table for what she calls standard markon.

Expenses	25%	0.25
Markdowns	6%	0.06
Stock shortages	1%	0.01
Employee discounts	3%	0.03
Alteration costs	2%	0.02
Profit	10%	0.10

1. Find the total initial standard markon percent.

2. If an item has a sales price of $10.00 with standard markon, what was the cost price?

3. If an item has a cost price of $8.80, what will be the selling price based on the standard markon?

4. Out of a total planned sales volume of $26,000, what amount must be deducted for employee discounts?

5. What is the planned amount to cover expenses out of a sales volume of $20,000?

An item is purchased for $26.40.

6. What is the selling price if the standard markon is applied?

7. What is the new selling price if, after two months, the average markdown is applied?

SINGLE ITEM AND MULTIPLE PRICING

To encourage sales, retailers sometimes set a price for one item and also a price for two or three identical items. This second price represents a lower price for the individual item.

For example, a shirt store or department might sell one shirt for $8.00 and two shirts for $15. When you enter such a store, you might be planning to buy one shirt. But when you see that there is a small savings when purchasing two shirts, you might decide to spend the extra money and, in a sense, "save" money.

In order to be sure that the markon is sufficient, a buyer might establish the multiple price according to required markon percents and then establish the single item price by working up from the multiple item price. In other cases, the multiple item price might be established by a markdown of the original price.

Example:

A buyer priced men's sport shirts at $9.95 each, 3 for $28.00.

a. How much less is the price of three shirts purchased at the multiple price than purchased individually?

b. Find the price if a customer buys five shirts.

Solution:

a. $3 \times 9.95 = 29.85$

$$29.85 - 28.00 = 1.85$$

Three shirts cost $1.85 less when purchased at the multiple price.

b. Five shirts cost:

28.00	Cost of three shirts
+19.90	Cost of two individual shirts.
47.90	

PRACTICE 10.2

A buyer has established the following prices:

A package of tennis socks (2 pairs in a package), $4.50.

A can of tennis balls, $2.95.

A bag of golf tees, $1.50.

Tennis shirts, $7.95 each; two for $15.00.

Golf balls: three for $5.00; a dozen for $18.00.

Find the cost of each of the following.

1. Two packages of tennis socks.

2. Two cans of tennis balls.

3. Two bags of golf tees.

4. Two tennis shirts.

5. Fifteen golf balls.

6. An order including all of the items in 1 through 5, above.

A buyer prices men's socks at 79¢ a pair, three pairs for $2.25. At the end of the day, sales records indicate $246.48 of individual unit sales, and $330.75 of multiple sales.

7. Find the number of individual unit sales.

8. Find the number of multiple unit sales.

9. If the tennis socks received an original markon of 40%, what was the cost per package to the retailer?

10.3 EXPENSES AND MARKUP

In Chapter 9 you studied the various types of expenses that a retailer incurs in running a business and that a retailer must consider when establishing prices. The two key elements in markup (the initial markon) are expenses and profit. You have seen, however, that expenses include many costs. Some of these costs can be anticipated and some may come as surprises.

Retailers must base markup on planned expenses and profit. If expenses are fewer than the plan calls for, then profits will be greater.

Example:

An item costs $10.00. Planned expenses per item are $6.00 and the retailer wants to earn a profit of $2.00.

a. Find the selling price.

b. Find the percent markup.

Solution:

a. The selling price equals the cost plus markup: $10 + 6 + 2 = 18$.

b. The percent markup is found by dividing the markup by the selling price:

$$8 \div 18 = 0.444 = 44.4\%$$

PRACTICE 10.3

An item costs $100.00. The total planned expenses are $20.00, and the expected profit is $5.00.

1. Find the total dollar markup.

2. Find the retail prices necessary after including the markup and profit.

3. Find the markup percent.

A retailer plans to establish a price of $220.00 for men's suits. The expenses are planned at $85.00, and the expected profit is $20.00.

4. Find the most that the retailer can pay for the suit and still cover the planned expenses and expected profit.

5. Find the markup percent.

CHAPTER TEST

A retailer establishes the following table of markdown categories. He uses this table for what he calls standard markon.

Expenses	27.5%
Markdowns	4.5%
Stock shortages	1.0%
Employee discounts	2.5%
Alteration costs	2.0%
Profit	9.0%

1. Find the total initial standard markon percent.
2. If an item has a sales price of $13.50 with standard markon, what was the cost price?
3. If an item has a cost price of $66.00, what will be the selling price based on the standard markon?
4. Out of a total planned sales volume of $15,000, what amount must be deducted for employee discounts?

A buyer has established the following prices:

Shirts, two for $25.00; 1 for $13.00

T-shirts, three for $14.00; 1 for $5.00

Socks, two pairs for $7.00

Find the cost of each of the following:

5. Four shirts.
6. Four T-shirts.
7. Six pairs of socks.
8. Two shirts and three T-shirts.

An item costs $155. The total planned expenses are $75, and the expected profit is $25.

9. Find the retail prices necessary after including the markup and profit.
10. Find the markup percent.

ANSWERS

10.1	1.	47%
	2.	$5.30
	3.	$16.60
	4.	$780
	5.	$5,000
	6.	$19.81
	7.	$46.82

10.2	1.	$9
	2.	$5.90
	3.	$3
	4.	$15
	5.	$23
	6.	$55.90
	7.	312
	8.	147
	9.	$1.35

10.3	1.	$25
	2.	$125
	3.	20%
	4.	$115
	5.	47.7%

CHAPTER TEST

1. 46.5%

2. $7.22

3. $123.36

4. $375

5. $50

6. $19

7. $21

8. $39

9. $255

10. 39.2%

11 Cumulative Markon

The owners and managers of retail stores are interested not only in the markon for individual items such as shirts or shoes. More important, they want to know the markon of an entire inventory over a given period of time.

After completing this chapter you will be able to:

- Describe the different elements in cumulative markon.
- Use given data to find cumulative markon.
- Solve problems about cumulative markon.

We have seen that retail business managers record all of their purchases, sales, and expenses as they occur. A business never stops keeping financial records. But at regular time intervals, usually monthly and quarterly (every three months), the business "closes the books" and looks at what has happened during that time.

11.1 CUMULATIVE MARKON

Cumulative markon is based on the total cost and selling price of goods available for sale during a particular time period, such as a month. This analysis over time is necessary if a business is to know whether or not it is achieving its goals. For example, a retailer may know that she must achieve a markon of 50% to pay expenses and earn a modest profit. But as inventory comes into the store at different costs and is sold at different prices, it may turn out that the cumulative markon for total inventory during one month is only 45%. After discovering this, the retailer can make changes in her business in order to achieve her goals.

Cumulative markon is an important element in the education and training of buyers. A buyer might be inclined to place a low markon on goods in order to encourage sales. It is, therefore, important for managers to inform buyers about markon policies. Some retail stores require that all buyers' purchase orders be approved by a division manager. Other stores require approval for exceptions to the markon policy.

VOCABULARY REVIEW

Net Purchases: Gross purchases minus returns to suppliers.

Net Additional Markups: Gross additional markups minus additional markup cancellations.

Transfers in: Merchandise purchased from another department or from another store.

Transfers out: Merchandise sold to another department or to another store.

To calculate cumulative markup:

1. Begin with the value of the opening inventory and add it to net purchases, transfers in, and net additional markups,

2. Subtract returns to suppliers, transfers out, and additional markup cancellations,

3. Calculate cumulative markon amount by subtracting the cumulative cost value of merchandise from the cumulative retail value,

4. Calculate cumulative percent markon by dividing cumulative markon by cumulative retail value.

Table 11–1 shows the steps and calculations needed to calculate cumulative markup.

TABLE 11–1

Calculating Cumulative Markup

1.	Cost Price	Retail Price
Opening Inventory	$54,000	$85,000
Net Purchases	16,000	24,000
Transfers In	3,000	5,000
Net Additional Markups		1,500
Subtotal	$73,000	$115,500
2.		
Returns to Suppliers	3,500	6,000
Transfers Out	1,000	1,500
Total	$68,500	$108,000

3. Cumulative Markon = Retail Price − Cost Price

$$= 108,000 - 68,500 = 39,500$$

The cumulative markon is $39,500.00.

4. Cumulative Markon Percent = Cumulative Markon ÷ Retail Price

$$= 39,500 \div 108,000 = 36.6\%$$

The cumulative markon percent is 37%.

PRACTICE 11.1

J. H. Goldfarb Company owns a chain of shoe stores. For the month of January, one store had an opening inventory with a cost price value of $50,000 and a retail price value of $75,000. There were net purchases with a cost price of $9,500 and a retail price of $13,000. Net transfers in had a cost price of $5,000 and a retail price of $8,000. Net additional markups amounted to $2,000. Returns to suppliers had a cost value of $2,000 and a retail value of $3,000. Net transfers out had a cost price of $3,500 and a sale price of $7,000. Complete Table 11–2 to find the total cost price and total retail price.

TABLE 11–2

Practice for Calculating Total Cost Price and Total Retail Price

1.	Cost Price	Retail Price
Opening Inventory	1. _____	2. _____
Net Purchases	3. _____	4. _____
Transfers In	5. _____	6. _____
Net Additional Markups		7. _____
Subtotal	8. _____	9. _____
2.		
Returns to Suppliers	10. _____	11. _____
Transfers Out	12. _____	13. _____
Total	14. _____	15. _____

16. Find the cumulative markon.

17. Find the cumulative markon percent.

11.2 NET PURCHASES

In calculating cumulative markon, the term *net purchases* has been used. It is important at this point to consider what is included in this amount.

We have seen in previous chapters that the total of an invoice, sometimes called gross purchase or gross invoice cost of merchandise, can include the invoice cost of goods, certain taxes, vendor charges for services such as labeling, and transportation charges. The total of these, as applicable in particular circumstances, yields the gross purchase amount.

Net purchase is obtained by subtracting certain amounts from the gross purchase amount. Among these deductions are returns to vendors, allowances from vendors, and rebates from vendors. Returns include the cost price of goods shipped back for full credit. Allowances are amounts granted by the vendor for late delivery, faulty merchandise, or wrong goods. A rebate is an amount paid by a supplier to a retailer in return for the purchase of an agreed upon quantity. The sum of these amounts comprises the total reductions of purchases. This sum is subtracted from the gross purchase amount to find net purchases.

Example:

A shipment of merchandise arrives from a vendor at a company's distribution center. The gross purchase cost of the shipment is $72,000. After the shipment is received and the goods are inspected, there are returns of $10,000, allowances of $2,000, and rebates of $1,000.

Find (a) the total reductions of purchases and (b) the net purchase.

Solution:

a.	Returns to vendors	$10,000
	Allowances from vendors	2,000
	Rebates from vendors	1,000
	Total reductions of purchases	$13,000
b.	Gross purchase cost	$72,000
	Total reductions of purchases	13,000
	Net purchases	$59,000

PRACTICE 11.2

A shipment of goods arrives from a vendor. The gross purchases amount is $30,000. There are returns to the vendor totalling $3,000 and allowances from the vendor of $1,200.

1. Find the total reductions of purchases.

2. Find the net purchases.

A shipment of merchandise has a gross purchases amount of $36,000. There are transportation charges of $1,000, a returns to vendor amount of $2,400, and allowances from the vendor of $1,000.

3. Find the total gross purchases.

4. Find the total reductions of purchases.

5. Find the total net purchases.

For the month of February, the Globe Department Store had an opening inventory with a cost price value of $110,000 and a retail price value of $180,000. There were gross purchases with a cost price of $21,000. There were returns to vendors of $3,500 and a rebate of $500. The retail price of the net purchases was $30,000. Net transfers in had a cost price of $3,000 and a retail price of $6,000. Net additional markups amounted to $3,500. Returns to suppliers of items already in stock and priced had a cost value of $4,000 and a retail value of $6,000. Net transfers out had a cost price of $3,000 and a sale price of $5,000. Complete Table 11–3 to find the total cost price and total retail price.

TABLE 11–3

Calculating Total Cost Price and Total Retail Price

1.	Cost Price	Retail Price
Opening Inventory	6. _____	7. _____
Net Purchases	8. _____	9. _____
Transfers In	10. _____	11. _____
Net Additional Markups		12. _____
Subtotal	13. _____	14. _____
2.		
Returns to Suppliers	15. _____	16. _____
Transfers Out	17. _____	18. _____
Total	19. _____	20. _____

21. Find the cumulative markon.

22. Find the cumulative markon percent.

CHAPTER TEST

During the month of March, Adrienne Chernov, a retailer, purchased total cumulative merchandise with a cost price of $19,000, and a sales price of $38,000.

1. Find the cumulative markon.

2. Find the cumulative markon percent.

A retail store has merchandise with a cumulative retail price of $60,000 and a cumulative cost price of $40,000.

3. Find the cumulative markon.

4. Find the cumulative markon percent.

A retail store has the following records for a month: Net additional markups, $2,000; net transfers in, $1,000 at cost and $1,500 at retail; net purchases, $10,000 at cost and $20,000 at retail; opening inventory, $20,000 at cost and $30,000 at retail.

5. Find the total cumulative cost price.

6. Find the total cumulative retail price.

7. Find the cumulative markon.

8. Find the cumulative markon percent.

A store has a cumulative merchandise retail price of $36,000 and a cumulative markon of $12,000.

9. Find the cumulative markon percent.

For the month of May the Sporting Center store had an opening inventory with a cost price value of $80,000 and a retail price value of $130,000. The net purchases had a retail value of $22,000 and a cost value of $12,000. Net transfers in had a cost price of $2,000 and a retail price of $3,500. Net additional markups amounted to $1,500. Returns to suppliers had a cost value of $7,000 and a retail value of $14,000.

Net transfers out had a cost price of $5,500 and a sale price of $9,000. Complete the table below to find the total cost price and total retail price.

1.	Cost Price	Retail Price
Opening Inventory	10. _____	11. _____
Net Purchases	12. _____	13. _____
Transfers In	14. _____	15. _____
Net Additional Markups		16. _____
Subtotal	17. _____	18. _____
2.		
Returns to Suppliers	19. _____	20. _____
Transfers Out	21. _____	22. _____
Total	23. _____	24. _____

25. Find the cumulative markon.

26. Find the cumulative markon percent.

ANSWERS

11.1
1. $50,000
2. $75,000
3. $9,500
4. $13,000
5. $5,000
6. $8,000
7. $2,000
8. $64,500
9. $98,000
10. $2,000
11. $3,000
12. $3,500
13. $7,000
14. $59,000
15. $88,000
16. $29,000
17. 33%

11.2
1. $4,200
2. $25,800
3. $37,000
4. $3,400
5. $33,600
6. $110,000
7. $180,000
8. $17,000
9. $30,000
10. $3,000
11. $6,000
12. $3,500
13. $130,000
14. $219,500
15. $4,000
16. $6,000
17. $3,000
18. $5,000
19. $123,000
20. $208,500
21. $85,500
22. 41%

CHAPTER TEST

1. $19,000
2. 50%
3. $20,000
4. 33.3%
5. $31,000
6. $53,500
7. $22,500
8. 42%
9. 33.3%
10. $80,000
11. $130,000
12. $12,000
13. $22,000
14. $2,000
15. $3,500
16. $1,500
17. $94,000
18. $157,000
19. $7,000
20. $14,000
21. $5,500
22. $9,000
23. $81,500
24. $134,000
25. $52,500
26. 39.2%

12 Markdown

You know from experience that the prices of goods can go down as well as up. We often say, "I think I'll wait until it goes on sale." Markdown is the name given to the amount or percentage of reduction in the price of an item.

After completing this chapter you will be able to:

- Explain the reasons for markdown.

- Find the amount and percentage of markdown for given situations.

- Solve realistic problems related to markdown.

- Understand the use of markdown in advertising.

12.1 REASONS FOR MARKDOWN

A markdown in prices permits a retailer to sell excess merchandise. This becomes particularly important when goods are damaged or shopworn. Retailers also want to move stock when they are left with small quantities of items that do not fit well with the rest of the store's goods. At certain times, such as when seasons change, retailers also want to clear out large quantities of stock in order to make room for items that will be in demand and that will realize a greater profit.

A second reason for markdown involves competition and promotion. When retail stores sell identical or nearly identical items they try to win customers from one another by setting lower prices.

A third reason for markdown is to correct errors. A buyer may have purchased too many of a particular style, color, or size—or the workmanship may be inferior. A store will then try to sell the excess merchandise at lower prices.

Markdown is calculated as a percent of selling price. Markdown can be considered for a particular item or for an amount of inventory.

Example 1:

A store has planned net sales of $95,000 for June. The planned markdown is 10%.

    a. What will the markdown amount be?

    b. What will the net sales with the markdown be?

Solution:

    a. Net Sales × Markdown Percent = Markdown Amount

$$95,000 \times 10\% = 9,500$$

    b. Planned Net Sales − Markdown Amount = Revised Net Sales

$$95,000 - 9,500 = 85,500$$

Example 2:

A shirt with a selling price of $20.00 is given a markdown of $3.00. Find the markdown percent.

Solution:

Markdown Amount	÷	Old Selling Price	=	Markdown Percent	
3	÷	20	=	0.15	= 15%

■ PRACTICE 12.1

1. What are two reasons that retailers use markdown?

The Men's Department of the Globe Department Store has $15,000 planned net sales for August. A markdown of 8% is put in place.

2. Find the markdown amount.

3. Find the revised net sales amount.

The merchandise plan for the handbag department calls for a markdown allowance of 13% for a six-month period. The projected net sales for the period are $500,000.

4. Find the dollar markdown for the six-month period.

5. Find the revised projected net sales.

A sweater selling for $25.00 is given a new selling price of $21.00.

6. Find the markdown amount.

7. Find the markdown percent.

Pairs of shoes have a cost price of $40.00 and a selling price of $75.00. When some of the shoes do not sell, they are marked down $10.00.

8. Find the original markup amount.

9. Find the original markup percent.

10. Find the markdown percent.

12.2 MARKDOWN ALLOWANCE

A retailer who plans ahead will project merchandise costs, sales goals, expenses, and profits. From these figures the retailer will know the amount and percent that he can allow for markdowns.

For example, if the total markdown allowance amount for the month of May is $5,000 and as of May 20 a buyer has taken $3,500, then the remaining amount that may be taken in markdowns is $1,500.

Example:

The Ocean View Fishing Supply Store plans net sales for August to be $50,000. The planned markdown is 8%. By August 20 the store manager had taken $2,300 in markdowns. Find the dollar amount of markdowns that can still be taken in August.

Solution:

Net Sales × Markdown Percent = Markdown Amount
50,000 × 8% = 4,000

Markdown Allowance − Amount Taken = Amount Remaining
4,000 − 2,300 = 1,700

The store can put into effect $1,700 in additional markdowns.

CANCELLATIONS OF MARKDOWN

A markdown in the price of an item or a class of items may be put into effect and later cancelled. Advertisements sometimes say, "Sale—One Day Only." In such a case, everything in a store might be marked down 30% for Presidents' Day, then the prices will return to what they were before the sale.

The following should be noted about markdown cancellations:

A cancellation applies to the same items that received the markdown.

The effect of a cancellation cannot exceed the markdown amount.

The following equation is used for markdown amounts or percents.

Gross Markdown − Cancellation of Markdown = Net Markdown

Example:

A buyer reduced 100 hats from $20.00 to $15.00 for a sale. At the sale price, 75 hats were sold. The remaining 25 hats were repriced at $25. Find:

a. The original markdown percent per hat.

b. The total gross markdowns.

c. The total markdown cancellation.

d. The total net markdowns.

e. The total additional markups.

Solution:

a. The markdown amount is 20 − 15 = 5; the markdown percent is 5 ÷ 20 = 25%.

b. The total gross markdown is 100 × $5.00 = $500.00.

c. The total markdown cancellation depends on the markdown amount and the number of items remaining. The markdown cancellation is $5.00. The number of items is 25.

$$\$5.00 \times 25 = \$125.00$$

d. Total net markdown = Gross Markdown − Cancellations

$$= \$500.00 - \$125.00 = \$375.00$$

e. The total additional markup can be determined by multiplying the number of items by the individual markup amount.

$$\$5.00 \times 25 = \$125.00$$

PRACTICE 12.2

The toy department in the Globe Department Store has planned net sales of $44,000 for the month of May. It also had a planned markdown of 10%. As of May 21, $2,700 in markdowns have been taken.

1. Find the planned markdown amount.

2. Find the amount of markdown that can still be taken.

The markdown amount allowance for the jewelry department in May is $12,800 on net sales of $160,000. As of May 21, the total amount of markdowns taken is $8,900.

3. Find the planned markdown percent.

4. Find the markdown amount remaining.

A buyer reduced the price of 50 bicycles from $80.00 to $70.00. At the end of the week, the remaining 5 bicycles were remarked to the original price.

5. Find the total gross markdown amount.

6. Find the total amount of the markdown cancellation.

7. Find the total net markdown.

A glove buyer is planning a one-day Saturday Special. She has decided that $14.99 will be the sale price. The following are the reductions:

Style A: 100 pairs reduced from $20.00 to $14.99.

Style B: 100 pairs reduced from $18.00 to $14.99.

Style C: 100 pairs reduced from $16.50 to $14.99.

The results of the sale were:

Style A: 75 pairs sold.

Style B: 88 pairs sold.

Style C: 93 pairs sold.

At the end of the day, the remaining pairs were remarked as follows:

Style A: $25.

Style B: $20.

Style C: $18.

8. Find the total gross markdown for Style A.

9. Find the total gross markdown for Style B.

10. Find the total gross markdown for Style C.

11. Find the total amount of the markdown cancellation for Style A.

12. Find the total amount of the markdown cancellation for Style B.

13. Find the total amount of the markdown cancellation for Style C.

14. Find the total net markdown for Style A.

15. Find the total net markdown for Style B.

16. Find the total net markdown for Style C.

17. Find the total additional markup amount for Style A.

18. Find the total additional markup amount for Style B.

19. Find the total additional markup amount for Style C.

20. Find the total amount of revenue if the remaining pairs of gloves of all styles are sold.

12.3 ACHIEVING MARKON PERCENT GOALS AND DOLLAR GOALS

Retail stores and departments within larger stores sometimes have to consider price changes in view of established goals. After a quantity of items has been sold, the retailer or buyer might have to ask what markdown is possible in view of the established goals.

Suppose that a department has a planned average markon goal of 36%. A buyer purchases 100 pairs of slacks at $12.00 a pair and assigns them a selling price of $20.00 a pair. After selling 80 pairs, he wants to know how much he can markdown the remaining pairs and still earn the 36% profit.

This problem must be performed in steps to answer the questions:

1. What is the planned markon amount?

2. What amount has been realized after the sale of 80 pairs?

3. What amount remains?

4. What is the remaining amount per pair?

5. What selling price is needed to earn the remaining amount?

1. What is the planned markon amount?

Recall the equation for cost, markon, and selling price percent:

Cost Percent + Markon Percent = Selling Price Percent
Cost Percent + 36% = 100%

Therefore, the cost percent is 64% of the selling price, and

(100 × 12) = 64% × Total Sales Amount
Total Sales Amount = 1,200 ÷ 64%
Total Sales Amount = $1,875.00

The markon goal is:

1,875 − 1,200 = 675

2. What amount has been realized after the sale of 80 pairs? The individual markon amount is $8.00, therefore:

8 × 80 = 640

3. What amount remains to be earned to achieve the goal?

675 − 640 = 35

4. What is the remaining amount per pair?

35 ÷ 20 = 1.75

5. The slacks can be marked down to $12.00 − $1.75 = $10.25

PRACTICE 12.3

A department has a planned average markon goal of 40%. A buyer purchases 120 shirts at $9.00 and assigns them a selling price of $16.00.

After selling 100 shirts, she wants to know how much she can markdown the remaining shirts and still earn the 40% profit.

12.4 SALES VOLUME TO ACHIEVE PLANNED GOALS

Percentages are used by retailers to gather and maintain information about sales figures and profits of many different items bought and sold at different prices. Markup and markdown percentages are used so that prices set by the buyer include amounts for expenses, profit, and any special needs. But, ultimately, when the time comes to pay its bills, retail stores and departments deal with money, not percentages. So at times a retailer will work out dollar goals for particular items to see if markdowns are likely to work.

A buyer purchases an item for $3.00 and places a retail price of $5.00 on it. The item sells at the rate of 100 per week. The buyer then considers a markdown of 10%, but she wants to know what sales volume will be necessary to achieve the same total dollar markon amount as the $5.00 price.

To find the needed sales quantity with the new markon:

1. Find the total markon amount at the original price.

2. Find the individual markon amount at the new price.

3. Divide to find the sales quantity at the new price.

1. The markon amount is $5 - 3 = 2$.

With sales of 100 per week, the markon amount is $200.00.

2. The markdown of 10% means $10\% \times 5.00 = \$0.50$. Therefore, $\$5 - 0.50 = \$4.50$, the new price, and $\$4.50 - \$3.00 = \$1.50$, the individual markon amount.

3. $200 \div 1.5 = 133.3$.

At the new price of $4.50, the store will have to sell 134 units. We round the number up in order to surpass the $200.00 amount.

PRACTICE 12.4

1. A buyer purchases an item for $5.00 and places a retail price of $8.00 on it. The item then sells at the rate of 120 per week. The buyer then considers a markdown of 15%. Find what sales volume is necessary to achieve the same total dollar markon amount as the $8.00 price.

2. A retailer purchases umbrellas for $8.00 and places a retail price of $15.00 on them. The umbrellas then sell at the rate of 30 per week. The retailer then considers a markdown of 10%, but she wants to know what sales volume will be necessary to achieve the same total dollar markon amount as the $15.00 price.

CHAPTER TEST

1. What are two reasons for the use of markdown?

The Home and Garden Center had $30,000 planned net sales for June. A markdown of 7% is put in place.

2. Find the markdown amount.

3. Find the revised net sales amount.

The merchandise plan for the building supply department calls for a markdown allowance of 12% for a six-month period. The projected net sales for the period are $48,000.

4. Find the dollar markdown amount allowed for the six-month period.

5. Find the revised projected net sales.

A shovel selling for $18.00 is given a new selling price of $14.00.

6. Find the amount of the markdown.

7. Find the markdown percent.

A pet store has planned net sales of $30,000 for the month of April. It also had a planned markdown of 8%. As of May 21, $1,300 in markdowns have been taken.

8. Find the planned markdown amount.

9. Find the amount of markdown that can still be taken.

A retailer has a planned average markon goal of 40%. She purchases 70 calculators at $50.00 each and assigns them a selling price of $90.00. After selling 55 calculators, she lowers the price and sells the remaining 15 calculators for $75 each.

10. Find the total dollar markon needed to earn a 40% markon at the $90 price.

11. Find the markon amount achieved at the two sales prices and volumes.

12. A buyer purchases an item for $4.00 and places a retail price of $7.00 on it. The items then sell at the rate of 100 per week. The retailer then considers a markdown of 20%, but he wants to know what sales volume will be necessary to achieve the same dollar markon as the $7.00 price.

ANSWERS

12.1
1. Answers will vary. Possible answers: to sell excess merchandise, to make room for new inventory, to attract customers.
2. $1,200
3. $13,800
4. $65,000
5. $435,000
6. $4
7. 16%
8. $35
9. 46.7%
10. 13.3%

12.2
1. $4,400
2. $1,700
3. 8%
4. $3,900
5. $500
6. $50
7. $450
8. $501
9. $301
10. $151
11. $125.25
12. $36.12
13. $10.57
14. $375.75
15. $264.88
16. $140.43
17. $125
18. $24
19. $10.50
20. $4,828.44

12.3 The remaining 20 may be sold for $10.00 each.

12.4
1. 200 items per week
2. 39 umbrellas per week

CHAPTER TEST

1. Sell items more quickly; attract customers to the store.

2. $2,100

3. $27,900

4. $5,760

5. $42,240

6. $4.00

7. 22.2%

8. $2,400

9. $1,100

10. $2,520

11. $2,575

12. 188 items per week

13 Stock Shortages

A few years ago universal product codes (UPC) did not exist. Now they appear on most of the items you purchase in food stores and many other stores. The UPC sends information about an item into a computer and allows the retailer to maintain up-to-the-minute inventory information.

There are a variety of business factors and conditions to be reviewed when considering expenses. Small losses can make a big difference in profits. This is why retail stores must keep careful records of stock.

After completing this chapter you will be able to:

- Explain the relationship of stock shortages to profit.

- Explain the meaning of physical inventory.

- Solve realistic problems about stock shortage.

Stock refers to the items that retailers buy and sell. A book store might have 2,000 books in stock. A sports store might have 20 or 30 of many different kinds of items in stock—bats, balls, skates, athletic shoes, T-shirts, socks, and much more.

Another term for stock is *merchandise inventory*. The word "merchandise" means that these items are the ones that are bought and sold to earn profits for the store. The store would have other inventory such as supplies of cleaning materials or computer paper. These are not sold for a profit but are needed to run the business. Often, when the meaning is clear, the word *inventory* alone is used for merchandise inventory.

Whether it is a large chain or a single small store, a retailer's success depends on sales with profit. Therefore it is important for a retailer to keep careful records of inventory and keep shortages as low as possible.

There are several causes for a reported shortage of inventory. The first case is the physical loss of merchandise. This is the most serious form of shortage because it results in actual financial loss for the company or store. This loss can be because of breakage, over-weighing, theft by employees, or shoplifting. Retailers do their best to guard against each of these possible occurrences. Many clothing stores use tags that, if not removed from the garment, will set off an alarm when the item is taken outside the store.

A second source of reported inventory shortage occurs because of errors in paperwork. Mistakes can be made in writing orders, reading numbers, entering numbers into a computer, and performing computations. Buyers, salespersons, and clerical help must be trained to work carefully and, as appropriate, to check one another's work.

A third source of errors is in taking physical inventory, that is, in determining the actual number of items in stock. Through the use of universal product codes, stores are now able to maintain a continuous update of actual inventory.

Retail stores often operate on small profits and thus even small stock shortages can hurt. Suppose, for example, a store has profits that amount to 5% of net sales and it is discovered that the store has a stock shortage caused by shoplifting of items that costs the store $100. If that $100 must be paid for from profits, then:

$$5\% \times \text{Net Sales} = \$100$$
$$\text{Net Sales} = \$100 \div 0.05 = \$2,000$$

It will therefore take $2,000 in sales to earn profits of $100 that will cover the lost caused by theft.

DOLLAR INVENTORY SHORTAGE

Retailers maintain records of the actual numbers of items in stock. But they are most concerned about the dollars that these items represent. For consistency with other expenses, retailers generally consider the retail value of inventory. (For tax purposes, the cost value is used.)

A chain of retail stores will generally try to maintain an inventory shortage that is lower than 2% of net sales. Thus, for example, if net sales total $400,000, the cost of inventory shortage should be kept under $8,000.

The *book inventory* is the amount of stock in dollars that is on hand, monitored by a perpetual inventory system. A *perpetual inventory system* maintains continuous records and updates the inventory figures daily or, at least, frequently. Under this system, sales, markdowns, and discounts (to employees or to other special groups) are deducted from the total purchases to date. The word "book" refers to the amount of retail inventory that the records indicate should be on hand.

The following terms, that you have seen and have used before, are used in calculating shortage and book inventory:

Net Sales: Gross sales minus returns from customers.

Net Markdowns: Gross markdowns minus markdown cancellations.

Net Reductions: Total of markdowns, special discounts, and shortages.

Deductions: Net sales plus reductions.

To determine the book inventory, it is necessary to find the value of total merchandise handled in a given time period. This will include opening inventory plus purchases, transfers, and markups. From this total value, whatever decreases the value must be subtracted, that is, sales, markdown, discounts, and shortages.

In the following, all figures are considered at retail.

Opening Inventory	$10,000	
Additions at Retail		
Net Purchases	25,000	
Transfers In	1,000	
Net Additional Markups	500	
Total Merchandise Handled		$36,500

Deductions at Retail

Net Sales	$20,000	
Net Markdowns	3,000	
Employee and Other Discounts	1,000	
Total Deductions from Retail		$24,000
Ending Book Inventory at Retail		$12,500

These figures indicate that the total retail value of inventory, before sales or markdowns, was $36,500. As a result of sales to customers, markdowns, and other reductions, there should be an inventory of goods with a retail sales value of $12,500.

Suppose that the physical inventory has a retail value of $11,700. Since the physical inventory is the actual amount and it is less than the book inventory, there is an inventory shortage:

Book Inventory − Physical Inventory = Inventory Shortage
12,500 − 11,700 = 800

As a percent of net sales, the shortage is:

800 ÷ 20,000 = 0.04 = 4%

If the book physical inventory is greater than the book inventory, then there is said to be an overage. An overage is usually a result of a clerical error.

PRACTICE 13.1

The book inventory for a toy store is $150,000. The physical inventory is $145,500.

1. Is there an inventory shortage or overage?

2. What is the amount of the shortage or overage?

The following figures are all given at retail:

Opening inventory	$20,000
Net purchases	5,000

Net additional markups	1,000
Net sales	12,000
Net markdowns	5,000
Discounts	1,000
Physical inventory	7,700

3. Find the dollar total of merchandise handled.

4. Find the total reductions.

5. Find the total deductions.

6. Find the book inventory.

7. Find the dollar shortage or overage.

8. If there is a shortage, find it as a percent of net sales.

The following figures are all given at retail:

Opening inventory	$50,000
Net purchases	6,500
Net additional markups	1,000
Net sales	25,500
Net markdowns	3,500
Discounts	1,000
Physical inventory	27,900

9. Find the dollar total of merchandise handled.

10. Find the total deductions.

11. Find the book inventory.

12. Find the dollar shortage or overage.

13. If there is a shortage, find it as a percent of net sales.

13.2 ACTUAL COST OF SHRINKAGE

Shrinkage, which is another word for the shortages we have been discussing, is measured in retail sales dollars so that it can be seen as a percent of retail sales along with other expenses—all being measured in the same way.

In real dollars, however, when a shortage occurs, a store only loses the cost of the items, not the retail sales amounts.

If a shortage occurs through the loss of a number of different items such that the cost is difficult to determine, the cumulative markon percent can then be used to determine the cost.

Example:

A total dollar shortage of $5,000.00 is found. The cumulative markon is 40%. Find the cost value of the shortage.

Solution:

Cost Percent + Markon Percent = Sales Percent (100%)
Cost Percent + 40% = 100%
Cost Percent = 60%

Cost Percent = 60% × $5000 = $3000

PRACTICE 13.2

1. The retail value of a shortage is $10,000. The cumulative markon percent is 30%. Find the cost value of the shortage.

Net sales for a large store equal $400,000. Shortage is 1.5% of net sales. The cumulative markon rate is 35%.

2. Find the shortage amount in sales dollars.

3. Find the shortage amount in cost dollars.

Shortage in sales dollars for a store is $1,200. Shortage is 2% of net sales. The cumulative markon rate is 40%.

4. Find the net sales amount.

5. Find the shortage amount in cost dollars.

CHAPTER TEST The book inventory for a store is $105,000. The physical inventory is $104,000.

1. Is there an inventory shortage or overage?

2. What is the amount of the shortage or overage?

The following figures are all given at retail:

Opening inventory	$35,000
Net purchases	15,000
Net additional markups	3,000
Net sales	32,000
Net markdowns	7,000
Discounts	2,000
Physical inventory	11,400

3. Find the dollar total of merchandise handled.

4. Find the total reductions.

5. Find the total deductions.

6. Find the book inventory.

7. Find the dollar shortage or overage.

8. If there is a shortage, find it as a percent of net sales.

Net sales for a large store equal $200,000. Shortage is 2.5% of net sales. The cumulative markon rate is 40%.

9. Find the shortage amount in sales dollars.

10. Find the shortage amount in cost dollars.

ANSWERS

13.1 1. Shortage
2. $4,500
3. $26,000
4. $6,000
5. $18,000
6. $8,000
7. $300 shortage
8. 2.5%
9. $57,500
10. $30,000
11. $27,500
12. $400 shortage
13. 1.6%

13.2 1. $7,000
2. $6,000
3. $3,900
4. $60,000
5. $720

CHAPTER TEST

1. Shortage

2. $1,000

3. $53,000

4. $9,000

5. $41,000

6. $12,000

7. $600

8. 1.9%

9. $5,000

10. $3,000

14 Stock Turnover

In Chapter 13 you learned that retailers must monitor inventory and try to prevent stock shortages. These shortages create an expense that is in fact a loss of money for the store. In this chapter we will discuss the frequency with which inventory passes through a retailer's storage.

After completing this chapter you will be able to:

- Explain the meaning and importance of turnover.

- Solve problems about turnover.

- Explain why a higher turnover increases profits.

It may at first seem that it does not matter whether a store or company keeps a large or a small amount of inventory, as long as the items are in stock when needed: This is not true because keeping inventory costs money. First, a store has to pay for the inventory. Second, it has to pay for space by buying or renting storerooms and warehouses. Third, with large amounts of inventory, a retailer runs the risk of having excess stock. Items may go out of style, or may be replaced by improved types, or customer demand might not be as great as was anticipated. Finally, retail stores must pay taxes on inventory. For all of these reasons, retailers try to keep the level of stock at a reasonably low level. But, of course, they do not want the level of stock to get so low that the merchandise is depleted and goods are unavailable when customers want them.

14.1 AVERAGE INVENTORY

The amount of inventory in any warehouse or storeroom varies from month to month and even from day to day. The graph in Figure 14–1 shows the amount of inventory, valued in retail dollars, for the first day of each of six months.

The amount of inventory is unknown for any days other than the ones shown. Sales of products cause inventory to decrease; purchases of goods from suppliers cause inventory to increase. So on any given day the amount of inventory could be virtually anywhere on the graph. But we can find an average inventory by taking the average of the inventory on the first day of each month. There are six months, so the amounts are added in thousands and are divided by six.

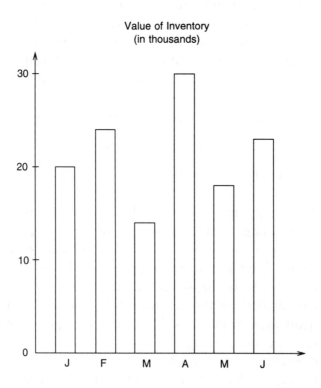

FIGURE 14.1

$$\text{Average} = (20 + 24 + 14 + 30 + 18 + 23) \div 6 = 129 \div 6 = 21.5$$

The average inventory for these six months, therefore, is $21,500.

Average inventory is similar to the average level of a lake. Whether you take measurements once a month or once a day, the meaning of the average does not change. But the accuracy of your average will vary depending on how many measurements you use. Using computers, companies can now obtain inventory figures each day and can easily calculate the average inventory based on these daily figures.

PRACTICE 14.1

1. Give two reasons why retailers do not want to have too much stock in inventory.

2. Why would a retailer not want to have too little stock.

A retailer's records show the following inventory for the first day of each of six months:

July	$45,000
August	37,500
September	41,300
October	56,800
November	47,200
December	53,700

3. Find the average inventory based on the first two months.

4. Find the average inventory based on the six months, rounded to the nearest hundred dollars.

5. Draw a bar graph showing the given inventory data.

14.2 TURNOVER

A ratio is a comparison of two numbers using division. You are already familiar with many different ratios. For example, miles per hour is a ratio. If you travel 200 miles in 5 hours, your average speed is 40 miles per hour.

Turnover per year, or *turn*, as it is sometimes called, is the ratio of net sales per year to average inventory in retail dollars.

For example, if a store has annual net sales of $100,000 and an average inventory of $20,000 its yearly turnover is:

$$\text{Net Sales} \div \text{Average Inventory} = \text{Turnover}$$
$$100,000 \div 20,000 = 5$$

You can think of turnover as the number of times a store empties out its inventory. In the previous example, if the store lets its inventory go down to zero and then ordered $20,000 worth of merchandise, it would go through this process five times.

Turnover can be calculated by numbers of items, retail value, or cost value. For example, a car dealer might have an inventory of 50 cars and sell 100 cars a year. Thus the dealer's turnover, in items, is 2. If, for the same situation, the net sales are $1.5 million and the average inventory is $900,000 then the turnover based on retail value is 1.7.

Turnover varies widely among different types of merchandise and different retail operations. A food store has a high turnover, but most antique shops have a relatively low turnover.

Most larger retail stores establish turnover goals as an aid to planning and monitoring sales. The turnover indicates to the retailer whether a particular department's or the entire store's merchandise is moving from the shelves, tables, showcases, and racks into the customers' hands according to the established turnover goals. By improving turnover, a retailer can improve the store's efficiency and profits.

PRACTICE 14.2

The Uptown Car Dealership maintains an average inventory of 74 cars. Last year 185 cars were sold. Last year net sales were $2.6 million and the average inventory at retail was $950,000.

1. Find the turnover based on number of items.

2. Find the turnover based on retail value.

Last year Rob's Clothing store had annual net sales of $264,000. Its inventory for the beginning of each month for the first half of the year follows:

January	$45,000
February	38,700
March	56,200
April	51,300
May	65,400
June	47,600

3. Find the average inventory.

4. Find the annual turnover, rounded to the nearest tenth.

14.3 INCREASING TURNOVER

Sometimes, in order to increase the efficiency of a retailing operation, a company or store will try to increase its turnover. There are only three ways to do this: (1) decrease the average inventory while maintaining the same level of sales, (2) increase sales while maintaining the same level of inventory, or (3) decrease average inventory and also increase net sales. To achieve greater accuracy, in this section we round turnover to the nearest hundredth.

Example 1:

The Footloose Shoe Company had an average inventory of $40,000 for year one of their expense-cutting plan. The net sales for the year were $150,000. For year two, the president wants the average inventory to be cut to $36,000 while maintaining sales at the same level.

a. Find the increase in turnover.

b. Find the percent increase in turnover.

Solution:

a. Turnover for year one: 150,000 ÷ 40,000 = 3.75
   Turnover for year two: 150,000 ÷ 36,000 = 4.17
   Increase in turnover: 4.17 − 3.75 = 0.42

b. Using the year one turnover as the base:
   Percent turnover = 0.42 ÷ 3.75 = 0.112 = 11.2% increase

Example 2:

The Footloose Shoe Company achieved its turnover goal exactly as planned, which is something companies almost never do. So for year three, the president wants to increase sales to $160,000 while maintaining the same average inventory.

a. Find the increase in turnover from year two to year three.

b. Find the percent increase in turnover from year two to year three.

c. Find the percent increase in turnover from year one to year three.

Solution:

a. Turnover for year two, found in Example 1, is 4.17
   Turnover for year three: 160,000 ÷ 36,000 = 4.44
   Increase in turnover: 4.44 − 4.17 = 0.27

b. Using year two as base
   Percent turnover = 0.27 ÷ 4.17 = 0.065 = 6.5%

c. Turnover increases from year one to year three: 4.44 − 3.75 = 0.69
   Using the first year as base: 0.69 ÷ 3.75 = 0.184 = 18.4%

PRACTICE 14.3

The Sporting Life Company had an average inventory of $60,000 for year one of their improvement plan. The net sales for the year were

$230,000. For year two, the plan calls for a cut in the average inventory to $52,000 while maintaining sales at the same level.

1. Find the turnover for year one.

2. Find the projected turnover for year two.

3. Find the percent increase in turnover if the plan is successful.

The Sporting Life Company was not successful in its efforts to decrease average inventory. In fact the average inventory increased from $60,000 to $65,000.

4. Find the turnover for year two.

5. Find the decrease in turnover.

6. Find the percent decrease in turnover.

P. J. Nickel Stores had annual net sales of $2,560,000. The store's inventory for the beginning of each month for the first half of the year follows:

January	$720,000
February	670,000
March	685,000
April	744,000
May	590,000
June	650,000

7. Find the average inventory.

8. Find the turnover.

9. The president wants to increase the turnover to 4. What percent increase would that be?

10. What average inventory will yield a turnover of 4 if sales are maintained at the current level?

11. What increase in sales will yield a turnover to 4 if average inventory is maintained at the current level?

The Home and Garden Center had an average inventory of $75,000 and annual sales of $230,000. The following year, average inventory decreased by 10% and sales increased by 10%.

12. Find the turnover for the first year.

13. Find the turnover for the second year.

CHAPTER TEST

1. List two reasons why it is important for a company or store to control its quantity of inventory.

2. What is turnover?

A retailer's net sales for a year are $110,400. Records show the following inventory for the first day of each of six months:

July	$28,000
August	33,500
September	17,300
October	34,800
November	35,800
December	24,600

3. Find the average inventory based on the first two months.

4. Find the average inventory based on the six months shown.

5. Draw a bar graph showing the given inventory data.

6. Find the turnover based on retail value.

Harry's Hardware Store had annual net sales of $164,000. His inventory for the beginning of each month for the second half of the year follows:

July	$55,000
August	29,700
September	47,300
October	50,200
November	34,600
December	38,700

7. Find the average inventory rounded to the nearest hundred dollars.

8. Find the annual turnover.

9. If sales for the following year increase to $175,000 while average inventory remains unchanged, find the turnover for that year.

10. Find the percent increase in turnover from the first to the second year.

14.1 1. Maintaining inventory is an expense; items might go out of style and not sell.
2. A store does not want to be out of inventory when there is customer demand.
3. $41,250
4. $46,900
5. See graph below.

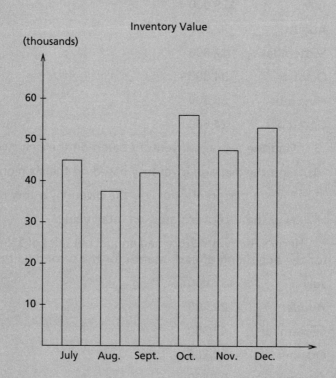

Inventory Value

14.2 1. 2.5
2. 2.7
3. $50,700
4. 5.2

14.3 1. 3.83
2. 4.42
3. 15.4%
4. 3.54
5. 0.29
6. 7.6%
7. $676,500
8. 3.78
9. 5.8%

10. $640,000
11. $2,706,000
12. 3.07
13. 3.75

CHAPTER TEST

1. To reduce expenses; to maintain stock levels that will satisfy customer demand.

2. Net sales divided by average stock value.

3. $30,750

4. $29,000

5. See graph below.

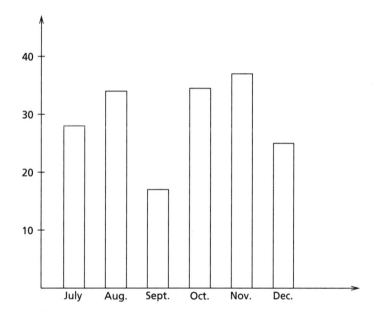

6. 3.81

7. $42,600

8. 3.85

9. 4.11

10. 6.8%

Part III Selling

15 The Merchandise Plan

To be successful, a retail business needs a plan. A plan is simply a statement of where you want to go and how you hope to get there. If, for example, you decide to make a trip by car from Philadelphia to Dallas, you have a destination. But there are many different roads you can take and places you can visit along the way. After deciding on the cities and other points of interest to visit, you would use a map to plan the route.

Selling is similar. You have to have financial goals and also have a kind of map telling how you hope to achieve the goals. This plan will state the number of different products that you will buy and sell. As time passes, you look at the sales plan and at actual sales to see whether you are going where you want to go.

After completing this chapter you will be able to:

- Explain why a merchandise plan is needed.
- Understand how to develop a merchandise plan.
- Use a spreadsheet to develop and check a merchandise plan.
- Solve problems related to a merchandise plan.

A good merchandise plan requires the participation of different people with various responsibilities. In a large store, many people will be involved, such as the president or manager, buyers, salespersons, advertising specialists, stock clerks, bookkeepers, and others. Each must do his or her job well for the business to succeed in following its plan and in making a profit. Most of what these people do comes under the heading of planning and controlling.

A merchandise plan, therefore, is a statement of objectives along with the methods that will be used to monitor the plan, that is, the methods used to determine at regular times whether the objectives are being achieved.

The merchandise plan will contain statements of each of the following items for each month, season, quarter, or year, depending on the nature of the business:

Total sales

Total E.O.M. inventory

Total reductions

Total purchases

Turnover

Stock–sales ratio

The following items may be included:

Markon percent

Gross margin

Stock shortage

Average inventory

Advertising costs

Payroll expense

Before establishing a merchandise plan, a business owner or manager must carefully review the purchases and sales that have been made during the previous months or year. These purchases and sales will indicate whether a plan is realistic. The larger goals will then be determined according to the categories mentioned previously. Finally, the responsibilities of buyers, sellers, and others will be established so that each person has his or her own goals and understands how they contribute to the achievement of the overall business. It is important, for example, for a buyer to know how much he or she can spend, what markon and mark-down percentages and amounts are acceptable, what sales levels are adequate, and what levels are outstanding. In other words, the plan lets the buyer know whether he or she is doing a good job.

You have seen in previous chapters that the spreadsheet is a powerful and useful computer program. The spreadsheet is particularly well suited for maintaining financial records; in today's world hardly any business would want to be without one.

In addition to being an ideal way to list various financial categories, the spreadsheet can be used with many built-in formulas that automatically produce totals, averages, and percentages. If a number is changed in one cell, then any totals or other amounts that depend on that cell will be automatically revised using the new number.

The spreadsheet in Figure 15–1 shows many of the financial figures for a three-month merchandise plan.

Each category of the spreadsheet contains:

1. Last year's financial figures (LY)

2. Planned figures for this year

3. Actual figures for this year, which will be filled in month by month

The categories are:

Sales at listed prices with markup. These prices are used to maintain a consistent base for calculating and comparing markup, sales ratio, and turnover.

Stock amount stated in retail dollars

End of month stock-to-sales ratio, that is, stock divided by sales

Reductions, including markdowns, discounts, and shortages

Purchases of items to be sold at retail value

Purchase markup in percent

Gross margin or revenue after deducting the cost of goods sold. This was explained in Chapter 8.

FIGURE 15–1

	A	B	C	D	E	F
		February	March	April	Total	Average
1						
2	Sales LY	38300	48700	39700	126700	42233.33
3	Plan	44000	52000	42800	138800	46266.67
4	Actual					
5	Stock EOM LY	84300	102300	87300	273900	91300
6	Plan	92400	98800	94200	285400	95133.33
7	Actual					
8	Stock/Sales Ratio	2.2	2.1	2.2		2.17
9	Plan	2.1	1.9	2.2		2.07
10	Actual					
11	Reductions LY	7300	4700	4400		5466.67
12	Plan	7700	5500	4700		5966.67
13	Actual					
14	Purchases LY	74900	71400	29100	175400	58466.67
15	Plan	94100	63900	42900	200900	66966.67
16	Actual					
17	Markup LY	0.427	0.429	0.418		0.42
18	Plan	0.45	0.45	0.45		0.45
19	Actual					
20	Gross Margin LY	12200	18200	14000	44400	14800
21	Plan	15500	20400	16700	52600	17533.33
22	Actual					

PRACTICE 15.1

Use the spreadsheet to answer the following questions. Some questions can be answered by simply finding data on the spreadsheet. For others, calculations must be performed.

1. What were the net sales for March of last year?

2. What are the planned net sales for March?

3. Find the amount of increase in sales from March of last year to March of the plan.

4. Find the percent of increase in sales from March of last year to March of the plan.

5. What was the stock-to-sales ratio for April of last year?

6. What does this ratio mean?

7. What was the average markup for the three months covered in the report?

8. If actual sales for February are 10% higher than the plan, what will they be?

9. If the actual gross margin for the three months is 10% lower than the plan, will it be higher or lower than last year?

10. What is the percent of increase from last year's average gross margin to the plan?

15.2	# MONITORING A MERCHANDISE PLAN

A merchandise plan is monitored or controlled by finding the actual figures for each month and comparing them with the merchandise plan and with the previous year's figures.

Actual sales figures for the merchandise plan shown previously are as follows:

February	$43,200
March	50,900
April	43,100

End-of-month actual stock figures are as follows:

February	$90,500
March	94,700
April	95,100

Percent reductions and purchase amounts were as follows:

	Reductions	Purchases
February	5.9%	$92,100
March	5.7%	67,400
April	4.7%	35,600

Gross Margin figures are as follows:

February	$14,800
March	$19,500
April	$17,000

PRACTICE 15.2

Use a computer spreadsheet program or construct a table as needed to answer the following. Use the data presented in the lesson.

1. Find the actual total sales for the three months.

2. Find the percent increase or decrease of the total sales from the total sales in the plan.

3. Enter the stock figures. Find the total and average stock for the three months.

4. Find the E.O.M. actual sales-to-stock ratio for each month.

5. Find the average gross margin amount for the three months.

6. Is the total actual gross margin greater or less than the plan?

7. Find the total gross margin difference between the plan and actual.

8. Find the gross margin percent of actual above or below the plan.

9. Which month had the highest actual sales as a percent of the plan?

FIGURE 15-2

	A	B	C	D	E	F
1		May	June	July	Total	Average
2	Sales LY	39600	33100	22700		
3	Plan	41600	35200	24000		
4	Actual					
5	Stock EOM LY	99000	82800	93100		
6	Plan	91500	84500	96000		
7	Actual					
8	Stock/Sales Ratio	2.5	2.5	4.1		
9	Plan	2.2	2.4	4		
10	Actual					
11	Reductions LY	4800	4900	4700		
12	Plan	4700	5200	4000		
13	Actual					
14	Purchases LY	56100	21800	37700		
15	Plan	43600	33400	39500		
16	Actual					
17	Markup LY	0.432	0.441	0.44		
18	Plan	0.45	0.45	0.45		
19	Actual					
20	Gross Margin LY	14400	11900	7400		
21	Plan	16100	13000	8600		
22	Actual					

CHAPTER TEST

The spreadsheet in Figure 15–2 shows figures for May, June, and July.

1. Find the totals and averages for the categories for which totals are appropriate.

2. For which categories did you not find totals and averages?

   Actual sales are as follows:

   May $43,700

   June   32,400

   July   29,800

3. For which months are actual sales higher than the plan?

4. What are actual sales in June, given as a percent of the plan.

   Gross margin amounts are as follows:

May	$16,400
June	10,700
July	9,300

5. Which month has the greatest actual gross margin?

6. Which month has the greatest gross margin as a percent of the plan?

7. Find the total actual gross margin amount.

ANSWERS

15.1
1. $48,700
2. $52,000
3. $3,300
4. 6.8%
5. 2.2
6. Average stock for April divided by net sales for Aprils is 2.2.
7. 42%
8. $48,400
9. Higher
10. 18.5%

15.2
1. $137,200
2. 1.2%
3. Total $280,300 average, $93,400
4. Stock-to-Sales Ratio: February 2.1, March 1.9, April 2.2
5. $17,100
6. Less
7. $1,300
8. 2.5% below
9. April

CHAPTER TEST

1. (See Spreadsheet on page 200)

2. Stock-to-Sales Ratio and Markup %

3. May and July

4. 92%

5. May

6. July

7. $36,400

FIGURE 15–2 Answer

	A	B	C	D	E	F
1		May	June	July	Total	Average
2	Sales LY	39600	33100	22700	95400	31800
3	Plan	41600	35200	24000	100800	33600
4	Actual					
5	Stock EOM LY	99000	82800	93100	274900	91633.33
6	Plan	91500	84500	96000	272000	90666.67
7	Actual					
8	Stock/Sales Ratio	2.5	2.5	4.1	2.9	2.9
9	Plan	2.2	2.4	4	2.7	2.7
10	Actual					
11	Reductions LY	4800	4900	4700	14400	4800
12	Plan	4700	5200	4000	13900	4633.33
13	Actual					
14	Purchases LY	56100	21800	37700	115600	38533.33
15	Plan	43600	33400	39500	116500	38833.33
16	Actual					
17	Markup LY	0.432	0.441	0.44		
18	Plan	0.45	0.45	0.45		
19	Actual					
20	Gross Margin LY	14400	11900	7400	33700	11233.33
21	Plan	16100	13000	8600	37700	12566.67
22	Actual					

16 Planning Sales

You have read a lot in earlier chapters about plans and planning. You would not take a long automobile trip without consulting a road map, and you cannot run a business without a plan. But you can't buy a ready-made plan the way you can buy a road map. So what is the basis for a sales plan?

After completing this chapter you will be able to:

- Understand and explain net sales.

- Explain the different approaches to planning sales.

- Solve problems related to net sales and sales plans.

- Analyze practical situations about sales plans.

16.1 A BASIS FOR PLANNING

Net sales is the amount of money that a store receives from customers after markdowns, returns, and other deductions are taken. The net sales amount is the base upon which other important figures, such as gross margin, are calculated. But how is the net sales figure planned? There are a variety of approaches and most businesses use a combination of several.

History

There is a saying sometimes used in business: "Ready, fire, aim." This means that it is best to get started, notice what happens, and then make more careful plans. This approach can be useful because it encourages a business to get started. As you have seen, however, businesses always look at the previous year as they make plans.

Managers' Decision

Although no one likes to hear the reason, "Because I say so," it does sometimes happen that a manager will set goals without full consultation and without stating all the reasons for the decision. For example, "Next year all departments will plan a net sales increase of 6%." This is an example of top-down planning. In today's business environment it is more common for a manager to meet with buyers, sales persons, and others to establish mutually agreeable goals.

Net Sales Based on Square Feet

A store or department that has more space than another will have more room to display and store goods, will be able to present a greater variety of items, and will generally have higher rent and utility bills. For these reasons, it is logical to expect a larger store or department to achieve greater sales. But clearly the products must also be considered. For example, a women's hosiery department might earn $120 a square foot per month, while a jewelry department might earn $300 a square foot per month.

Average Number of Transactions

In any store, there will be a great range in the value of customers' purchases. One customer may leave a hardware store having spent $0.89 for nails; another may leave after spending $350.00 for power tools. But there is also an average sale amount, which might be $5.00. A store can generally figure that with more customers and more transactions, its net sales will increase. Thus a retail store might plan on an increased number of transactions as a means of increasing its sales and revenue.

In Chapter 14 we considered sales plans based on stock turnover. In future chapters we will consider other bases for planning sales. For the remainder of this chapter we look at the areas mentioned previously as bases for planning.

Last Year's Sales and Manager's Decisions

Table 16–1 shows net sales for a three-month period and planned sales for the same months, with a 6% increase.

TABLE 16–1

Sales in Thousands

	August	September	October
Last Year	15.2	21.1	18.7
Planned	16.1	22.4	19.8

PRACTICE 16.1

1. What is the meaning of net sales?

2. What are two different methods for analyzing and comparing net sales?

Table 16–2 shows sales for three months. In planning for this year's sales, the manager has set goals of 8% increases for each month. Find the planned sales goals.

TABLE 16–2

Sales in Thousands

	May	June	July
Last Year	87.4	98.6	76.5
Planned	3. _____	4. _____	5. _____

Table 16–3 shows last year's sales for different departments. Find the planned sales figures for this year if the following are the percentage increases for the goals: women's, 10%; men's, 7.5%; sports, 12%.

TABLE 16–3

Sales in Thousands

	Women's	Men's	Sports
Last Year	23.4	16.3	8.9
Planned	6. _____	7. _____	8. _____

Table 16–4 shows last year's and planned sales.

TABLE 16–4

Sales in Thousands

	May	June	July
Last Year	54.5	67.3	61.2
Planned	61.2	68.3	64.3

9. Find the percent increase for May.

10. Find the percent increase for June.

11. Find the percent increase for July.

16.2 PLANNING SALES BASED ON SQUARE FEET

The Men's Department at the Globe Department Store occupies a total of 5,000 square feet. Last year the dollar sales amount was $145 per square foot. This year's sales plan calls for $150 per square foot.
We want to find:

1. The net sales for last year.

2. The planned net sales for this year.

3. The planned increase for this year.

4. The percentage increase or decrease in sales.

1. Net sales for last year:

$$145 \times 5,000 = 725,000$$

2. Net sales for this year:

$$150 \times 5,000 = 750,000$$

3. Increase:

$$750,000 - 725,000 = 25,000$$

4. Percent increase:

$$25,000 \div 725,000 = 0.034 = 3.4\%$$

PRACTICE 16.2

The Women's Department at the Globe Department Store occupies a total of 6,500 square feet. Last year the dollar sales were $175 per square foot. This year's sales plan calls for $190 per square foot.

1. Find the net sales for last year.

2. Find the planned net sales for this year.

3. Find the amount of planned increase for this year.

4. Find the percentage increase or decrease in sales.

The Cosmetics Department occupies 1,200 square feet. Last year net sales for the Cosmetics Department reached $165,000.

5. Find the net sales per square foot.

6. If sales increase by 9%, what will the net sales be per square foot?

16.3 SALES PLANS BASED ON NUMBER OF TRANSACTIONS AND AVERAGE SALE

Using the net sales and the total number of transactions, a store or company can calculate the average sale amount. This average sale amount can then be used in planning. For example, suppose that the average sale in the Leather Goods Department last year was $25.00 and that there were 15,000 transactions. This year's sales plan calls for an average sale of $30.00 and 16,000 transactions.

We want to know:

1. The dollar net sales realized last year.

2. The dollar net sales planned for this year.

3. The dollar increase or decrease planned for this year as compared with last year.

4. The percentage increase or decrease in sales of this year as compared with last year.

1. Last year's net sales:

$$\text{Average Sale} \times \text{Total Transactions} = \text{Net Sales}$$
$$25 \times 15,00 = 375,000$$

2. Planned sales:

$$\text{Average Sale} \times \text{Total Transactions} = \text{Net Sales}$$
$$30 \times 16,000 = 480,000$$

3. Dollar increase:

$$\text{Planned Sales} - \text{Last Year's Sales} = \text{Increase}$$
$$480,000 - 375,000 = 105,000$$

4. Percent increase:

$$\text{Increase} \div \text{Base} = \text{Percent Increase}$$
$$105,000 \div 375,000 = 28\%$$

PRACTICE 16.3

The average sale in the Shoe Department last year was $45.00 and there were 12,000 transactions. This year's sales plan calls for an average sale of $50.00 and 13,000 sales.

1. Find the dollar net sales realized last year.

2. Find the dollar net sales planned for this year.

3. Find the dollar increase or decrease planned for this year as compared with last year.

4. Find the percentage increase or decrease in sales this year as compared with last year.

5. The Sports Department had net sales last year of $162,400 and 12,400 transactions. Find the amount of average sale.

6. Find the net sales if there is planned increase of 10% in the number of transactions and 5% in the average sale.

7. The average sale in the Ladies Belt department last year was $7.00. This year the planned average sale is $8.00. Last year the department handled 20,000 transactions. This year 18,000 transactions are planned. Find the percent increase or decrease in the dollar planned net sales of this year as compared with last year.

TABLE 16–5

Sales in Thousands

	May	June	July
Last Year	12,300	14,600	13,200
Planned	1. _____	2. _____	3. _____

CHAPTER TEST

Table 16–5 shows sales for three months. In planning for this year's sales, the manager has set goals of an 8% increase for each month. Find the sales goals, rounded to the nearest hundred dollars.

The Kitchen Department at the Globe Department Store occupies a total of 5,500 square feet. Last year the dollar sales were $165 per square foot. This year's sales plan calls for $180 per square foot.

4. Find the net sales for last year.

5. Find the planned net sales for this year.

6. Find the planned increase for this year.

7. Find the percentage increase or decrease in sales.

The Jewelry Department occupies 900 square feet. Last year net sales for the Jewelry Department reached $190,000.

8. Find the net sales per square foot.

9. If sales increase by 4.5%, what will be net sales per square foot?

The average sale in the Electronics Department last year was $55 and there were 14,000 transactions. This year's sales plan calls for an average sale of $60 and 15,000 sales.

10. Find the dollar net sales realized last year.

11. Find the dollar net sales planned for this year.

12. Find the dollar increase or decrease planned for this year as compared with last year.

13. Find the percentage increase or decrease in sales of this year as compared with last year.

ANSWERS

16.1   1. Total amount paid by customers after subtracting returns, markdowns, and other deductions

2. Number of square feet for a store or department; number of transactions

3. 94.1
4. 106.5
5. 82.6
6. 25.7
7. 17.5
8. 10
9. 12.3%
10. 1.5%
11. 5.1%

16.2   1. $1,137,500
2. $1,235,000
3. $97,500
4. 8.6%
5. $137.50
6. $149.88

16.3   1. $540,000
2. $650,000
3. $110,000
4. 20.4%
5. $13.10
6. $187,618.2
7. 2.9% increase

CHAPTER TEST

1. $13,300

2. $15,800

3. $14,300

4. $907,500

5. $990,000

6. $82,500

7. 9.1%

8. $211.11

9. $220.61
10. $770,000
11. $900,000
12. $130,000
13. 16.9%

17 Planning Stocks

The previous chapter explained that sales can be planned in various ways. But no matter what method is used, it is most important that every retail business do the following: first, develop a plan; second, watch to see whether the business is achieving the objectives in its plan; third, change the plan when needed.

Sales are not the only part of a business for which plans are important. Stocks or inventory are also important. If a business has too much inventory then it may not have money available for other needs, or it may not sell all of its stock. If a business does not have enough inventory then it may not be able to meet its customers' needs and will lose business.

After completing this chapter you will be able to:

- Understand stock-to-sales ratio planning.

- Understand the importance of minimum stock quantity and reorder amounts.

- Understand the different ordering systems.

- Solve problems related to the different ordering systems, including the stock-to-sales planning, the model levels, and the week's supply ordering method.

17.1 PLANNING INVENTORY BASED ON STOCK-TO-SALES RATIO

Different kinds of consumer items require different kinds of stock planning. For some items there is a year-round, nearly constant demand. These items include household goods such as light bulbs, cleaning products, and many kinds of food. Personal products such as toothpaste also fall into this category. These items must be reordered from time to time in order to maintain a reasonable inventory.

Long-season items comprise the second type of consumer goods. Included in this category are gloves, seasonal sports equipment, and bathing suits. These items are purchased for a season and are reordered according to need during the season.

A third category of goods are the short-season items. These include decorations, cards, and gifts that are used for particular holidays or special events. These items are usually purchased only once, in quantities sufficient for the season.

A final category includes novelty and fashion items. These are usually purchased in small quantities, sometimes on consignment. The retailer then watches closely to see whether the style or novelty "catches on." He or she can then order more as needed.

The principles for ordering stock and maintaining inventory are the same for each of these four categories of goods, but they differ somewhat in implementation. In each case, the stock-to-sales ratio is a key indicator.

There are several different ways to calculate the stock-to-sales ratio. The first we shall consider is the B.O.M. (Beginning of Month) stock-to-sales ratio. You will recall that when working with stock figures, retailers generally use the retail value, that is, the selling price of items. This is what we will use in the stock-to-sales ratio.

Recall that a ratio is a relationship of two numbers using division. With this in mind we can define:

The *B.O.M. stock-to-sales ratio* is the ratio of the first-of-the-month retail inventory to the planned net sales for the month.

In fraction form this means:

$$\text{Stock-to-sales ratio} = \frac{\text{B.O.M. inventory}}{\text{Planned net sales}}$$

This equation can be solved for inventory or net sales by multiplying or dividing both sides of the equation as needed. Thus to find B.O.M. inventory, we multiply both sides by planned net sales and obtain:

B.O.M. inventory = (Stock-to-sales ratio) × (Planned net sales)

Planned net sales are found by multiplying both sides by the planned net sales and then dividing both sides by the stock-to-sales ratio:

$$\text{Planned net sales} = \frac{\text{B.O.M. inventory}}{\text{Stock-to-sales ratio}}$$

Example 1:

A retail store has a beginning-of-month (B.O.M.) stock of $30,000 and planned net sales of $7,500. Find the stock-to-sales ratio.

Solution:

The stock-to-sales ratio is found using the formula:

$$\text{Stock-to-sales ratio:} = \frac{\text{B.O.M. inventory}}{\text{Planned net sales}} = \frac{30,000}{7,500} = 4$$

Example 2:

A department store's B.O.M. stock is $201,400. Net sales are $64,700. Find the stock-to-sales ratio.

Solution:

Using the stock-to-sales ratio and a calculator with the decimal selector set at 2 yields:

$$\frac{\text{B.O.M. inventory}}{\text{Planned net sales}} = \frac{201,400}{64,700} = 3.11$$

Example 3:

A retailer wants to maintain a stock-to-sales ratio of 4.5. Her planned net sales are $7,500. What should be her beginning-of-month inventory?

Solution:

We can find the planned net sales using the B.O.M. stock-to-sales ratio:

$$\frac{\text{B.O.M. inventory}}{\text{Planned net sales}} = \frac{\text{Inventory}}{7{,}500} = 4.5$$

To find inventory, we multiply both sides of the equation by 7,500.

$$\text{Inventory} = 4.5 \times 7{,}500 = 33{,}750$$

Her B.O.M. inventory should be $33,750.

Example 4:

A department store has B.O.M. inventory of $405,700. What should the net sales be if the store wants a stock-to-sales ratio of 3.2?

Solution:

We use the stock-to-sales ratio:

$$\frac{\text{B.O.M. inventory}}{\text{Planned net sales}} = \frac{405{,}700}{\text{N. S.}} = 3.2$$

To solve the equation, we first multiply both sides by net sales (N. S.):

$$405{,}700 = 3.2 \times \text{N. S.}$$

Next we divide both sides by 3.2.

$$\text{N. S.} = 405{,}700 \div 3.2 = 126{,}781 = 126{,}800$$
rounded to the nearest hundred.

Net sales should be $126,800.

PRACTICE 17.1

1. What problem might occur if a retailer has too little inventory?

2. What problem might occur if a retailer has too much inventory?

3. What is the stock-to-sales ratio?

4. What does B.O.M. stand for?

5. A retailer has inventory of $64,800 and planned net sales of $18,200. Find the B.O.M. stock-to-sales ratio, rounded to the nearest hundredth.

6. A store has net sales of $9,000 and wants to maintain a stock-to-sales ratio of 4. What should its inventory value be?

7. A department store has B.O.M. stock of $562,000. What should its net sales be in order to have a stock-to-sales ratio of 2.5?

Table 17–1 shows monthly stock-to-sales ratios for one year.

8. Which month has the lowest stock-to-sales ratio?

9. Why do you think that month has the lowest ratio?

10. If the store has sales of $45,000 in March, what is its B.O.M. inventory?

11. If the store has inventory of $215,600 in October, what are net sales, rounded to the nearest hundred dollars?

TABLE 17–1

Monthly Stock-to-Sales Ratios for
One Year

Month	Stock-to-Sales
February	5.47
March	4.40
April	5.16
May	5.14
June	4.74
July	5.35
August	4.65
September	5.04
October	4.83
November	4.14
December	2.30
January	6.51

Some retailers calculate the stock-to-sales ratio based on end-of-month (E.O.M.) inventory. The decision about whether to use B.O.M. or E.O.M. is based on accounting and record-keeping procedures, but the calculating of the stock-to-sales ratio is the same no matter which procedure is used.

12. A store has monthly sales of $4,500 and E.O.M. stock of $25,200. Find the E.O.M. stock-to-sales ratio.

13. A retailer has an E.O.M. stock-to-sales ratio of 3.75. The net sales are $24,500. Find the inventory value, correct to the nearest hundred dollars.

17.2 PLANNING INVENTORY BASED ON STOCK TURNOVER

Turnover was described in Chapter 14. Stock turnover is also a ratio, in fact it is a ratio that uses the same categories as the stock-to-sales ratio.

The stock-to-sales ratio uses figures for just one month; thus the stock value is greater than sales. A store must have more than one month's worth of stock on hand.

The turnover ratio compares sales to stock, usually for a year or a half-year. During this length of time sales are greater than stock. So the turnover number shows the number of times that stock must be replenished. As explained previously, average inventory is determined by totaling the inventory at different times, for example, every week or every day, and then averaging.

$$\text{Average turnover} = \frac{\text{Net sales}}{\text{Average inventory}}$$

This equation, like the stock-to-sales ratio, can be solved for each of the other terms.

$$\text{Net Sales} = (\text{Average inventory}) \times (\text{Average turnover})$$

and

$$\text{Average inventory} = \frac{\text{Net sales}}{\text{Average turnover}}$$

Example:

A retail store has annual net sales of $239,600 and stock turnover of 2.76. Find the store's average inventory.

Solution:

To find average inventory, use the equation:

$$\text{Average inventory} = \frac{\text{Net sales}}{\text{Average turnover}} = \frac{239,600}{2.76} = \$86,800$$

PRACTICE 17.2

1. What is the meaning of stock-to-sales ratio?

2. What time period is used for stock-to-sales ratio?

3. What is the turnover ratio?

4. What time periods are usually used for turnover ratio?

Table 17–2 shows inventory figures for the end of each month.

5. Find the average inventory for the six months.

6. Net sales for February were $31,900. Find the stock-to-sales ratio for February.

TABLE 17–2

Inventory Figures for the End of Each Month

Month	Inventory
February	102,400
March	98,800
April	94,200
May	104,500
June	106,000
July	89,300

7. Net sales for the 6-month season were $201,400. Find the half-year turnover.

8. Net sales of $256,500 are planned for the next six months. What should the average inventory be if the store wants a turnover of 2.50?

17.3 MODEL LEVELS

Retailers use different methods in ordering. Some retailers simply keep an eye on stock and when it appears to be running low, they reorder. This method can work fairly well as long as the owner or manager keeps a careful watch on the merchandise. But it is easy to miss something, and customers will be displeased if the store runs out of basic items.

Some retailers depend on vendors to call regularly or even visit the store to monitor sales and maintain an ordering system. This method can work for some items, but not many retailers want to turn over their businesses to their suppliers.

Many retailers use the model method for staple items. For this method to work effectively, there must be certain patterns of sales and ordering:

1. The product must have a nearly fixed rate of sale.

2. The retailer must have a regular reorder pattern, such as every week.

3. The delivery time must be reasonably predictable.

If these three factors exist then the retailer can determine a model level based on rate of sale, reorder period, turnaround time, and a safety factor. These are defined as follows:

Rate of sale: The number of units sold on average during a period (day, week, month).

Reorder period: The time between orders.

Turnaround time: The delivery time required by the supplier.

Safety factor: A number of units above normal requirements needed to cover emergencies such as breakdowns and storms.

The model level for a particular situation can be found by adding the amounts needed to cover turnaround time, reorder time, and the safety factor.

$$\text{Model level} = \text{Turnaround time (amount)} \\ + \text{Reorder time (amount)} \\ + \text{Safety factor (amount)}$$

Example 1:

A retailer's rate of sale for an item is 50 units per week. The turnaround time is one week. Reorders are written every week. A week's reserve or safety is planned.

Solution:

The 50 units per week is the key to finding the model level. Since each of the factors requires one week's supply, the equation is:

$$\text{Model level} = 50 + 50 + 50 = 150.$$

Thus in an average week 50 units will be sold and 50 will arrive on order. There will be enough stock on hand in case an order is late or in case a larger-than-usual supply is sold.

Sometimes, because of fluctuations in sales or in ordering patterns, it is necessary to determine the correct amount of stock to order so that the model level of stock can be reached.

Example 2:

There are 50 units of stock on hand and 50 units on order. The item sells at a rate of 100 units a week. The turnaround time is one week. The reorder period is two weeks. The safety factor is one week. Find the amount to order to reach the model level of stock.

$$\text{Model level} = \text{Turnaround time (amount)} \\ + \text{Reorder time (amount)} \\ + \text{Safety factor (amount)}$$

The item sells at the rate of 100 units per week. Therefore,

$$\text{Model level} = 100 + 200 + 100 = 400$$

But since there are 50 items on hand and 50 on order, it is only necessary to order 300 items.

PRACTICE 17.3

1. A popular cosmetic item sells at the rate of 200 units a week. Turnaround time is two weeks. Reorders are placed every two weeks. The safety factor is one week. Find the model stock level.

2. A brand of shampoo sells at the rate of 150 units per week. Reorders are placed every three weeks. The turnaround time is one week. The safety factor is two weeks. Find the model level of stock.

3. A regularly selling item has the following factors:

   There are 100 units on hand and 100 units on order.

   The safety factor is two weeks.

   The reorder period is three weeks.

   The turnaround time is two weeks.

   The rate of sale is 200 units a week.

   Find (a) the model level of stock and (b) the quantity to reorder.

4. The weekly rate of sale of an item is 500 units. Reorders are placed every four weeks. Turnaround time is one week and the safety factor is two weeks. There are 1,000 on hand and 500 on order. Find (a) the model level of stock and (b) the quantity to reorder.

17.4 WEEKS OF SUPPLY AND INVENTORY DECISIONS

To be successful in retail business, the store owner or manager must keep a watchful eye on stock. Depending on sales, a typical retailer may use the following four decisions regarding stock.

1. Watch the item.

2. Mark the item down.

3. Reorder the item.

4. Allow the item to sell out.

Table 17–3 shows inventory levels (inventory on hand), sales, weeks of supply, and the retailer's decisions. Weeks of supply is equal to the inventory on hand divided by the rate of sales per week. The model level method discussed in the previous section can be used to determine an appropriate weeks-of-supply level. Suppose that the retailer has determined that 10 weeks of supply is the level that he would like to maintain for items that are selling at a good rate.

The model inventory level for item 1 is 150. This is because the sales rate per week is 15 items and the model level is 10 weeks. Weeks of supply is higher than planned. The retailer can watch the inventory for this item. If sales remain on target, she will order up to the model level at the appropriate time.

Item 2 is below the planned weeks of supply, which is 10. The retailer decides to reorder.

Item 3 is selling at a slow rate with high weeks of supply. The retailer decides to mark down, hoping to improve sales.

TABLE 17–3

Inventory Levels and Retailer's Decisions

Item	Inventory on Hand 7–1	Sales 7–1/7–15	Inventory on Hand 7/15	Rate per Week	Weeks of Supply	Decision
1	300	30	270	15	18	Watch
2	250	50	200	25	8	Reorder
3	250	10	240	5	48	Markdown

Weeks of Supply Ordering Method

The various factors considered in the previous discussion are brought together in a system called the weeks-of-supply ordering method. This method involves several steps.

1. The retailer must determine an ordering period. This might be a season of 26 weeks, a shorter holiday season, or some other length of time in weeks.

Along with the season, the retailer will decide on a stock turnover. As you have seen the stock turnover is the number of times that the stock of a particular product line sells during a period. This number is often between 2.5 and 6.

The number of weeks in a planning period divided by the planned stock turnover is equal to the amount of planned inventory based on weekly sales.

$$\frac{\text{Number of weeks}}{\text{Turnover}} = \text{Number of Weeks of Supply}$$

Suppose, for example, that a season of 26 weeks is the planning period and a turnover of 4 is planned. Then,

$$26 \div 4 = 6.5$$

This means that the store should keep 6.5 weeks of inventory on hand.

2. The retailer must next determine the average amount of sales per week. This amount, as in most planning, is in retail dollars and is generally a matter of history. A retailer finds, for example, that he or she is selling $800 worth of shirts per week. This amount is then used as the model inventory or weeks-of-supply level.

Average Weekly Sales $\times$ Weeks of Supply = Model Inventory

For the example above we have average weekly sales of $800 and weeks supply of 6.5.

$$800 \times 6.5 = 5,200$$

The retailer's model inventory level is $5,200.

3. The retailer's order will be determined by the amount of stock on hand and the model inventory level.

Model inventory $-$ Stock on hand = Order Amount

Suppose that the retailer has $3,700 worth of sweaters on hand, then he or she will order:

$$5,200 - 3,700 = 1,500$$

The order quantity is $1,500.

PRACTICE 17.4

Table 17–4 shows inventory on hand, two-week sales, rate of sales, and weeks of supply. The retailer's plan calls for 12 weeks of supply for each item. For each item write in the retailer's decision: watch, reorder, or markdown.

7. Write the reasons for your decision in number 1.

8. Write the reasons for your decision in number 3.

9. Write the reasons for your decision in number 5.

10. A retailer has a 26-week selling season and planned turnover of 3.5. What is his planned weeks of supply, rounded to the nearest week?

11. A retailer has planned weeks of supply of 8, inventory of $4,200, and average weekly sales of $900. How much inventory should she order to reach her model inventory level?

TABLE 17–4

Inventory on Hand, Two-Week Sales, Rate of Sales, and Weeks of Supply

Item	Inventory on Hand 7–1	Sales 7–1/7–15	Inventory on Hand 7/15	Rate per Week	Weeks of Supply	Decision	
4	250	25	225	12.5	19	1.	_____
5	214	32	182	16	11	2.	_____
6	200	35	165	17.5	10	3.	_____
7	200	10	190	5	38	4.	_____
8	148	1	147	0.5	294	5.	_____
9	148	8	140	4	25	6.	_____

A retailer has a 12-week holiday selling season and planned turnover of 2. He has average weekly sales planned at $1,800 and $4,700 of inventory on hand.

12. Find the planned weeks of supply.

13. Find the model inventory level.

14. Find the amount he should purchase.

CHAPTER TEST

1. What problem might occur if a retailer has too little inventory?

2. What problem might occur if a retailer has too much inventory?

3. A retailer has inventory of $84,000 and net sales of $20,000. Find the B.O.M. stock-to-sales ratio, rounded to the nearest hundredth.

4. A store has net sales of $6,500 and wants to maintain a stock-to-sales ratio of 4.5. What should its inventory value be?

5. A brand of soap sells at the rate of 300 units a week. Reorders are placed every two weeks. The turnaround time is two weeks. The safety factor is one week. Find the model level of stock.

6. A regularly selling item has the following factors:

There are 50 units on hand and 150 units on order.

The safety factor is two weeks.

The reorder period is two weeks.

The turnaround time is one week.

The rate of sale is 250 units a week.

Find (a) the model level of stock and (b) the quantity to reorder.
Table 17–5 shows inventory on hand, two-week sales, rate of sales, and weeks of supply. The retailer's plan calls for 12 weeks of supply for each item. For each item write in the retailer's decision: watch, reorder, or markdown.

TABLE 17–5

Inventory on Hand, Two-Week Sales, Rate of Sales, and Weeks of Supply

Item	Inventory on Hand 7–1	Sales 7-1/7–15	Inventory on Hand 7/15	Rate per Week	Weeks of Supply	Decision
1	350	60	290	30	9+	7. _____
2	200	40	160	20	8	8. _____
3	900	50	850	24	34	9. _____
4	200	20	180	10	18	10. _____

ANSWERS °

17.1   1. The retailer might run out of stock and might not be able to meet customer demand.
2. All of the stock might not sell.
3. Inventory ÷ Net Sales
4. Beginning of the Month
5. 3.56
6. $36,000
7. $224,800
8. December
9. Holiday sales lower inventory levels and this lowers the stock to sales ratio.
10. $198,000
11. $44,600
12. 5.60
13. $91,900

17.2   1. Stock ÷ Net Sales
2. One month
3. Net sales ÷ Average inventory
4. 6 months or 1 year
5. $99,200
6. 3.21
7. 2.03
8. $102,600

17.3   1. 1,000
2. 900
3. (a) 1,400, (b) 1,200
4. (a) 3,500, (b) 2,000

17.4   1. Watch
2. Reorder
3. Reorder
4. Markdown
5. Markdown
6. Watch
7. Sales are adequate; weeks of supply is slightly above plan.
8. Stock is under weeks of supply.
9. Sales are slow; weeks of supply is very high.
10. 7
11. $3,000
12. 6
13. $10,800
14. $6,100

CHAPTER TEST

1. May not be able to meet customer demand.

2. May not sell all of the stock.

3. 4.2

4. $29,250

5. 1,500

6. (a) 1,250; (b) 1,050

7. Reorder

8. Reorder

9. Markdown

10. Watch

18 Planning Purchases: Open-to-Buy

In the previous two chapters we discussed inventory, different ways of planning model levels of inventory, and methods for monitoring inventory. You learned that a retailer must not only buy and sell, but also check stock regularly and take appropriate action. Such actions include reordering in quantities needed, checking orders as they come in, and marking prices down to reduce stock.

But inventory management must also be seen in relation to sales. A retailer will be in financial trouble and perhaps will not even be able to proceed with business if he or she cannot pay all expenses. In this chapter we discuss purchasing as it relates to sales. We look at the methods a retailer must use to determine how much he or she can afford to spend on purchases at a particular time.

After completing this chapter you will be able to:

- Understand and explain the meaning of open-to-buy.

- Calculate open-to-buy based on given sales data.

- Calculate open-to-buy at cost.

- Understand the problems and remedies of overbuying.

- Solve problems related to open-to-buy situations.

OPEN-TO-BUY

"Open-to-buy" sounds strange but it is important to have a clear idea of exactly what it means. Study the following definition and return to it whenever you think you do not know the exact meaning of open-to-buy.

Open-to-buy is the amount of money that a retailer plans to spend on merchandise during a particular planning period.

Since the open-to-buy amount depends on the purchase plan, it is important that we consider the need for a purchase plan. A good purchase plan helps the retailer accomplish the following:

1. Maintain a proper balance between inventory and net sales.

2. Prevent unbalanced inventory.

3. Inhibit overbuying and impulse buying.

4. Diminish the likelihood of running out of stock.

5. Result in better turnover, fewer markdowns, and increased sales.

These ideas may sound familiar. In fact you may think that they were covered in the previous chapter when we discussed planning inventory. This is partly true, but the difference is that now we are considering all of the factors related to the cost of merchandise. A model inventory level may make sense based on considerations of turnover, ordering schedule, and delivery times, but the model inventory level may not be feasible with regard to the amount that a retailer is able to spend. Therefore, the open-to-buy method is another way to consider purchases.

You will recall that B.O.M. stands for Beginning of the Month, and E.O.M. stands for End of the Month.

Example 1:

A retailer has actual B.O.M. inventory of $50,000 for January and planned B.O.M. of $45,000 for February. These amounts are in sales dollars. During January she has projected sales of $30,000. What will be her January open-to-buy in preparation for the February B.O.M. merchandise level.

Solution:

The open-to-buy amount is found using two steps:

1. Find the projected E.O.M. based on sales.

$$\text{B.O.M.} - \text{Projected Sales} = \text{Projected E.O.M.}$$
$$50,000 - 30,000 = 20,000$$

The January E.O.M. is $20,000.

2. The open-to-buy is the amount that will bring the inventory level up to the planned B.O.M. for February.

$$\text{Planned Feb. B.O.M.} - \text{Projected Jan. E.O.M.} = \text{Open-to-Buy}$$
$$45,000 - 20,000 = 25,000$$

The open-to-buy is $25,000.

You must remember that, for the sake of consistency, the retailer works in sales dollars. But sales dollars are marked up from purchase amounts. So the retailer must work back to find the amount of real dollars that can be spent.

Example 2:

The retailer in Example 1 uses a standard markup of 40%. What will be her open-to-buy in purchasing dollars?

Solution:

Markup based on sales means that:

$$40\% \times \text{Sales} = \text{Markup Amount}$$

You have seen in earlier chapters that Markup + Cost = Selling Price. This is true both in dollars and in percent. Since the selling price is always 100%, the cost percent is:

$$100\% - \text{Markup \%}$$

In this case the cost percent is:

$$100\% - 40\% = 60\%$$

Therefore, to find the cost amount of open-to-buy, we multiply:

$$25,000 \times 60\% = \$15,000$$

PRACTICE 18.1

A retailer has an actual April B.O.M. of $80,000 and a planned May B.O.M. of $90,000. Sales in April are $32,000. His average markup is 45%.

1. Find his projected April E.O.M.

2. Find his April open-to-buy.

3. Find the open-to-buy in cost dollars.

A retail business has an actual June B.O.M. of $120,000 and a planned July B.O.M. of $110,000. Projected sales for June are $35,000. His markup is 50%.

4. Find the June open-to-buy.

5. Find the open-to-buy in cost dollars.

18.2 OTHER FACTORS IN THE OPEN-TO-BUY

In the examples and exercises above, the open-to-buy was considered only in relationship to merchandise levels and sales. There are other factors to be considered, such as orders placed during the month, markdown sales, stock shortages, cancellations, and discounts. These factors can be organized using two forms. One form extends and revises the B.O.M. figure; the other extends and revises the sales figures.

The B.O.M. inventory figure needs to be increased based on orders during the month.

You must remember that sales figures, as considered in the calculation of open-to-buy, are used to calculate how inventory levels have declined. Therefore, other factors that affect a decline in inventory must also be considered. These factors include sales at markdown levels, orders cancelled, and inventory returned to vendors. These taken together are called deductions and must, along with sales, be subtracted from B.O.M. in order to determine the projected E.O.M. amount.

Example 1:

The Cooper Carpet Company has a B.O.M. of $200,000 for September. During the month an additional order is placed for $35,000. Sales for the month are projected to be $60,000. Also during the month there are projected markdowns of sales amounting to $10,000. An order for $8,000 is cancelled and an incorrect shipment of $12,000 is returned to the vendor. Planned B.O.M. for October is $185,000. Find the open-to-buy amount.

Solution:

1. First find the adjusted B.O.M.:

$200,000   B.O.M.
+ 35,000   order
$235,000   adjusted B.O.M.

2. Next find the projected sales plus deductions:

$60,000   projected sales
10,000   markdown
8,000   cancellation
12,000   returns
90,000   total reductions

3. Subtract to find the projected E.O.M.:

$235,000   adjusted B.O.M.
− 90,000   total reductions
$145,000   projected E.O.M.

4. Subtract to find the open-to-buy:

$185,000 planned B.O.M.
  145,000 projected E.O.M.
$ 40,000 open-to-buy

Example 2:

If the Cooper Carpet Company uses a standard markup of 35%, what is the open-to-buy in cost dollars?

Solution:

If the markup amount is 35% of sales, then the cost is 65% of sales.

$$40,000 \times 65\% = 26,000$$

The open-to-buy cost amount is $26,000.

PRACTICE 18.2

The Home Fixit Company has a B.O.M. of $100,000 for October. During the month an additional order is placed for $15,000. Sales for the month are projected to be $30,000. Also during the month, there are projected markdown sales of $7,500. An order for $3,000 is cancelled. Planned B.O.M. for November is $110,000. The Home Fixit Company uses a standard markup of 40%.

1. Find the adjusted B.O.M.

2. Find the total reductions, including projected sales and other reductions.

3. Find the projected E.O.M.

4. Find the open-to-buy.

5. Find the open-to-buy in cost dollars.

18.3   OVERBUYING AND AMOUNT REMAINING IN THE OPEN-TO-BUY

The open-to-buy can tell buyers and managers what amount is available for purchases not only at the end of a month but on a continuing basis. Using the method already shown, you can compute the amount remaining in the open-to-buy for the balance of the month. The method will also tell the buyer if he or she has already overbought the open-to-buy.

Example 1:

The Casual Corner Clothing Store has a March B.O.M. of $40,000. The planned B.O.M. for March is $20,000. Additional orders for $10,000 are placed during March. Projected sales are $25,000. An order for $1,000 is cancelled. Find the open-to-buy, which in this case is an overbought situation.

Solution:

1. Find the adjusted B.O.M.:

$40,000   B.O.M.
+10,000   order
$50,000   adjusted B.O.M.

2. Find the projected sales plus reductions:

$25,000   sales
+ 1,000   cancellation
$26,000   total reductions

3. Subtract to find the projected E.O.M.:

$50,000   adjusted B.O.M.
−26,000   total reductions
$24,000   projected E.O.M.

4. Subtract to find the open-to-buy:

$20,000   planned B.O.M.
<u>−24,000</u>   projected E.O.M.
−$4,000   open-to-buy (overbought)

PRACTICE 18.3

The Home Fixit Company has a B.O.M. of $90,000 for May. During the month an additional order is placed for $10,000. Sales have been slow and as of May 15, sales for the month are projected to be $20,000. Also during the month, there are projected markdown sales of $2,000. An order for $1,000 is cancelled. Planned B.O.M. for June is $70,000. The Home Fixit Company uses a standard markup of 40%.

1. Find the adjusted B.O.M.

2. Find the total reductions, including projected sales and other reductions.

3. Find the projected E.O.M.

4. Find the open-to-buy, and tell whether it is an overbought situation.

5. Find the open-to-buy or overbought in cost dollars.

CHAPTER TEST

A retailer has an actual July B.O.M. of $60,000 and a planned August B.O.M. of $50,000. Sales in July are $20,000. The retailer's average markup is 45%.

1. Find the projected July E.O.M.

2. Find the open-to-buy.

3. Find the open-to-buy in cost dollars.

The Home and Garden Center has a B.O.M. of $20,000 for May. During the month an additional order is placed for $8,000. Sales for the month are projected to be $7,500. Also during the month, there are projected markdown sales of $1,500. An order for $2,000 is returned. Planned B.O.M. for June is $30,000. The Home and Garden Center uses a standard markup of 40%.

4. Find the adjusted B.O.M.

5. Find the total reductions, including projected sales and other reductions.

6. Find the projected E.O.M.

7. Find the open-to-buy.

8. Find the open-to-buy in cost dollars.

9. Explain what is meant by an overbought situation.

10. Why must a retailer know the open-to-buy in cost dollars?

ANSWERS

18.1	1.	$48,000
	2.	$42,000
	3.	$23,100
	4.	$25,000
	5.	$12,500
18.2	1.	$115,000
	2.	$40,500
	3.	$74,500
	4.	$35,500
	5.	$21,300
18.3	1.	$100,000
	2.	$23,000
	3.	$77,000
	4.	−$7,000
	5.	−$4,200

CHAPTER TEST

1. $40,000

2. $10,000

3. $5,500

4. $28,000

5. $11,000

6. $17,000

7. $13,000

8. $7,800

9. The End of Month exceeds the following month's planned Beginning of Month.

10. Cost dollars gives the actual amount that can be spent.

19 Pricing, Transactions, and the Average Sale

In the introduction to this book we talked about the four big ideas of retailing: buying, expenses, selling, and record keeping. Throughout the text you have seen that these four ideas are interrelated. We discussed pricing in Part I because as the retailer purchases products he is thinking about prices and whether the cost of goods will permit him to cover expenses.

We now discuss the topic of prices from a somewhat different perspective. We will consider pricing strategies and then the average sale. These are directly associated with the selling side of the business.

After completing this chapter you will be able to:

- Explain several different pricing strategies.

- Determine the average sale figure.

- Understand and explain strategies for increasing the average sale.

- Solve problems related to the average sale.

19.1 PRICING

In addition to markon discussed in Part I of this book, there are a number of other considerations with regard to pricing. First, the retailer must decide where he wants his prices to be with regard to the competition. *The competition* is a general term that refers to all of the businesses that sell similar products to the same general group of customers as the business that is making plans.

A retailer can set prices higher than, equal to, or lower than the competition. Setting higher prices is a way of telling customers that the products are of higher quality, are longer lasting, or that they have some prestige value.

Setting prices equal to the competition tells customers that the retailer will give as good a price as other stores. A retailer in this category may wish to compete in other ways, such as convenient locations, variety of merchandise, or customer service.

Setting prices lower than the competition lets customers know that they can get more for their money. Retailers using this strategy want to increase the number of customers to their stores and increase the volume of sales.

Another type of pricing is known as leader pricing, which means setting prices lower than the business's financial goals would usually permit. In fact, a *loss leader* is an item priced even below cost. Clearly a retailer can never make money selling below cost. But by pricing one or several items in this way, the retail businessperson hopes to attract and hold customers who will also buy products that are priced to make a profit.

The Average Sale

During the course of a month or a year, a retail store will have records of both the total dollar amount of sales and the total number of transactions. A *transaction* is a single sale, which could include one or several items purchased at the same time.

If a store has $1,000.00 in sales and 100 transactions, then clearly the average sale is $10.00. Some sales might have been for $50.00, and others might have been for $1.00 or less. But the average is $10.00.

The average sale is found by dividing total sales by the number of transactions.

Average Sale = Total Sales ÷ Number of Transactions

A retailer is interested in the average sale for a number of reasons. First, it may be that salespersons in the store are directing customers toward lower-priced items rather than trying to interest them in merchandise that costs a little more. Second, low average sale may indicate that the salespersons are not encouraging the customer to consider merchandise beyond what they had at first wanted to buy. Third, low average sale may mean that the store is out of stock on some items that are requested. Finally, low average sale may indicate that the products need to be presented in a more attractive way so that customers will be led to consider and make additional purchases.

Example:

A retail clothing store has sales of $12,000 in March and has had 650 transactions. Find the average sale amount.

Solution:

The formula for finding the average sale is:

$$\text{Average Sale} = \text{Total Sales} \div \text{Number of Transactions}$$
$$= 12,000 \div 650$$
$$= \$18.46$$

PRACTICE 19.1

1. What is meant by "the competition"?

2. Why might a retailer set prices above the competition?

3. What is a "loss leader"?

4. Why might a retailer use a loss leader?

5. A hardware store has monthly sales of $7,254 and has 1,060 transactions. Find the average sale.

6. A computer store has monthly sales of $10,988 and has 735 transactions. Find the average sale.

19.2 INCREASING THE AVERAGE SALE

You have seen in Chapter 16 that there are several possible ways to increase the average sale. The first way is to increase total sales while maintaining the same number of transactions. To do this, salespersons must make an extra effort to interest customers and to increase the amount of each sale. This approach might be used in a clothing store or in an all-purpose store.

A second strategy is to maintain the same amount of sales while decreasing the number of transactions. This approach might be used by a jewelry store or an automobile dealer. In these cases, the retailer could deliberately choose to sell higher-priced merchandise, even though it would result in fewer customers.

The third strategy to increase the average sale is both to increase total sales and also to reduce the number of transactions. This would combine the first two approaches and might be used by a gift or souvenir store that decided to raise the quality of its merchandise, knowing that the total number of transactions might decrease.

A fourth strategy is to increase sales while also increasing the number of transactions, but to increase sales by an amount such that the average sale also increases.

Example:

The Gilded Gift Shop had 20,000 transactions last year with sales of $80,000. This year the store plans to maintain the same level of sales with 18,000 transactions.

    a. Find the average sale for last year.

    b. Find the average sale for this year.

    c. What strategy is the retailer using to increase the average sale?

Solution:

    a. Last Year:

$$\text{Average Sale} = \text{Total Sales} \div \text{Number of Transactions}$$
$$= \$80,000 \div 20,000$$
$$= \$4.00$$

b. This Year:

Average Sale = Total Sales ÷ Number of Transactions
= $80,000 ÷ 18,000
= $4.44

c. The strategy is to maintain the sales level while reducing the number of transactions.

PRACTICE 19.2

A retail clothing store had sales last year of $20,000 and 500 transactions. This year the retailer plans to have sales of $25,000 with 500 transactions.

1. Find the average sale for last year.

2. Find the average sale planned for this year.

3. What strategy is the retailer using to increase the average sale?

A retailer had net sales of $50,000 last year and plans to increase the amount by 10% for this year. The retailer had 15,000 transactions last year and plans to have the same number for this year.

4. Find the average sale for last year.

5. Find the planned sales amount for this year.

6. Find the average sale planned for this year.

A retailer souvenir store had net sales last year of $75,000, with 25,000 transactions. This year it plans to increase the sales amount by 15% while increasing the number of transactions by 10%.

7. Find the average sale for last year.

8. Find the planned sales amount for this year.

9. Find the number of transactions planned for this year.

10. Find the average sale planned for this year.

11. Did the average sale increase or decrease from last year to this year?

12. What strategy was used?

THE NUMBER OF TRANSACTIONS

You have seen that retailers and business managers are always interested in percentages. This is because numbers alone can be deceiving. An increase of 100 transactions a month does not mean much until you know the nature of the business and the base on which the 100 transactions is built. For a hardware store with 2,000 transactions, an increase of 100 transactions is 5% and probably will not add more than 5% to the total sales. But for a car dealer with 100 transactions a month, an increase of 100 is 100%, which probably means that the sales amount will double.

Although in the previous sections of this chapter we discussed strategies in which a retailer might deliberately reduce the number of transactions, this practice is not common and would not commonly be recommended. Usually a store or business wants more customers, even if they are not spending large amounts of money.

Example 1:

A store has had 20,000 transactions this year and plans 25,000 for next year. What percentage of increase is the store planning?

Solution:

The increase in numbers is 25,000 − 20,000 = 5,000.

The base for the percent increase is this year's number, 20,000.

Percent is found by dividing the amount by the base:

$$5,000 \div 20,000 = 25\%$$

Example 2:

A department store had 75,000 transactions last year and plans to increase that number by 5% for this year. How many transactions does the store plan for this year?

Solution:

First find 5% of 75,000:

$$75,000 \times 5\% = 3,750$$

Then add the increase to the base:

$$75,000 + 3,750 = \$78,750$$

PRACTICE 19.3

1. The furniture department of a department store had 8,000 transactions last year. The plan calls for 10,000 transactions this year. Find the percent increase.

2. A food store had 23,000 transactions last year and plans an increase of 8% for this year. How many transactions does it plan for this year?

A car dealer had 300 transactions last year. Its plan for this year calls for an increase of 15 transactions.

3. How many transactions are planned for this year?

4. What percent increase is planned in transactions?

CHAPTER TEST

1. What is meant by *transaction?*

2. How do you find average sale?

3. A hardware store has monthly sales of $8,790 and 1,163 transactions. Find the average sale.

A retail gift store had net sales last year of $45,000, with 10,000 transactions. This year it plans to increase the sales amount by 10% while increasing the number of transactions by 5%.

4. Find the average sale for last year.

5. Find the planned sales amount for this year.

6. Find the number of transactions planned for this year.

7. Find the average sale planned for this year.

8. Did the average sale increase or decrease from last year to this year?

A clothing store had 3,000 transactions last year. Its plan for this year calls for an increase of 450 transactions.

9. How many transactions are planned for this year?

10. What percent increase is planned in transactions?

ANSWERS

19.1
1. Businesses selling the same or similar products to the same general group of customers
2. To emphasize quality, durability, and other product features
3. A product sold for a price that is below cost
4. To bring customers to the store or business
5. $6.84
6. $14.95

19.2
1. $40
2. $50
3. Increasing the total sales amount while maintaining the same number of transactions
4. $3.33
5. $55,000
6. $3.67
7. $3
8. $86,250
9. 27,500
10. $3.14
11. Increase
12. Increasing both the total sales amount and the number of transactions

19.3
1. 25%
2. 24,840
3. 315
4. 5%

CHAPTER TEST

1. A single sale
2. Divide the total net sales by the number of transactions
3. $7.56
4. $4.50
5. $49,500
6. 10,500
7. $4.71
8. Increase
9. 3,450
10. 15%

20 The Selling Cost Percent

A prominant United States senator, who was once a department store owner with extensive experience and a keen interest in retail business, said that when he went into a store to purchase socks or a tie he would be prepared to spend an additional $20.00 (perhaps $50.00 in today's dollars) if the salesperson would take the time and make the effort to bring an attractive and high quality product to his attention. But, he said, he rarely spent the $20.00 because the retailers almost never made the extra effort.

The owners or managers of retail stores are apt to pay a great deal of attention to the products that they buy and even more attention to the products that are good sellers. In this focus on purchases and sales they sometimes fail to appreciate the importance of good selling by their salespeople. It is important and necessary that the sales people be evaluated to see if they are contributing as they should be to the overall sales and profits.

After completing this chapter you will be able to:

- Understand and explain the meaning of selling cost.

- Understand and calculate selling costs for individuals and departments.

- Recognize and explain how selling cost affects profits.

- Solve practical problems about selling cost.

- Explain different types of promotional activities and explain the potential effect of promotion on productivity.

20.1 SELLING COST

In virtually every organization, company, or store, payroll is one of the greatest expenses. Even in a retail business that focuses on buying and selling, paying employees is a major expense.

Selling cost may be calculated based on an individual, a department, a store, or an entire organization. *Selling cost* is equal to payroll as a percent of net sales.

Selling Cost = Payroll Cost ÷ Net Sales

There are a variety of factors that can affect payroll cost. These include:

1. Salaries and wages paid. A retailer may save money by paying relatively low wages. But higher wages may attract more competent and motivated employees.

2. The amount or dollar value of sales. Increasing the volume of sales will increase the base for calculating selling cost and consequently will decrease selling cost as a percent.

3. Time spent in selling. Selling cost can be reduced if a particular product requires lengthy selling time or if an individual salesperson takes a long time completing each sale.

4. The location of the selling department. In a large department store, a location with greater access and visibility will generally attract more customers. Clearly, not every department can be on the first floor or near a door, so a manager will have to decide which departments will profit most from the better locations.

5. The ability of the salesperson. The success of a salesperson includes knowledge of the merchandise, the ability to assess a customer's needs and wants, and the ability to present a product so that it appears attractive when compared with the competition.

6. The size of a selling department. Customers do not like to be kept waiting, so it is important that a sales department have enough sales people to attend to each customer in a timely fashion.

7. The quality of merchandise. Products that are of high quality or that have virtually no competition may seem to sell themselves.

Example:

Marta Lopez is a salesperson in the dress department of a department store. She earns a weekly salary of $264.00. Her average weekly sales are $2,480.00. Find her selling cost.

Solution:

$$\text{Selling Cost} = \text{Payroll Cost} \div \text{Net Sales}$$
$$= 264 \div 2{,}480$$
$$= 10.7\%$$

PRACTICE 20.1

Find answers correct to the nearest tenth of a percent.

1. Gerald Glasser is paid $310 a week. His sales last week were $2,570. Find his selling cost.

2. Florence Lund is the buyer for the Infant's and Toddler's Apparel Department. Her planned selling cost for the department for February is 9.5%. Her planned net sales are $12,300. Find her wages.

3. The Furniture Department has a sales goal of $14,000 for March and a selling cost target of 12.5%. What will the sales cost be in dollars if the sales goal is achieved?

20.2 CHANGES IN THE SELLING COST

The selling cost is a ratio (that is, a fraction), which is then converted to a percent. The selling cost can therefore be decreased as any fraction can:

1. By increasing net sales while the payroll cost remains unchanged,

2. By decreasing the payroll cost while the level of net sales remains unchanged,

3. By increasing sales and also decreasing payroll costs.

Example:

Through the use of part-time employees, a buyer's payroll costs were reduced from $1,500 to $1,000 per month. The net sales remained at $20,000. Find

a. The selling cost percent with the $1,500 payroll,

b. The selling cost percent with the $1,000 payroll,

c. The decrease in the selling cost percent.

Solution:

a.

$$\text{Selling Cost} = \text{Payroll Cost} \div \text{Net Sales}$$
$$= 1,500 \div 20,000$$
$$= 7.5\%$$

b.

$$\text{Selling Cost} = \text{Payroll Cost} \div \text{Net Sales}$$
$$= 1,000 \div 20,000$$
$$= 5\%$$

c.

$$7.5\% - 5\% = 2.5\%$$

There has been a decrease of 2.5% in selling cost.

PRACTICE 20.2

Table 20–1 shows net sales for last year and this year, as well as payroll cost for last year and this year.

1. By looking at Table 20–1, determine which selling cost definitely increased from last year to this year.

2. By looking at Table 20–1, determine which selling cost definitely decreased from last year to this year.

3. Find the selling cost for housewares last year.

4. Find the selling cost for housewares this year.

5. Find the combined selling cost for the three departments last year.

6. Find the combined selling cost for the three departments this year.

7. Find the increase or decrease in selling cost from last year to this year.

TABLE 20–1

Net Sales and Payroll Cost

Department	Net Sales: Last Year	Net Sales: This Year	Payroll Cost: Last Year	Payroll Cost: This Year
Clothing	$71,400	$71,600	$8,700	$10,300
Housewares	$54,600	$48,200	$6,500	$5,900
Sports	$86,100	$94,300	$18,500	$17,500

20.3 PLANNED INCREASES IN SELLING COST

A retailer or department can plan decreases in selling cost by planning increases in net sales or by planning decreases in the payroll cost.

Example 1:

A retailer has March net sales of $23,000. Her payroll cost is $4,100. Find:

    a. The selling cost,

    b. The net sales needed to effect a 2% decrease in selling cost while keeping the same dollar payroll cost.

Solution:

    a. It is first necessary to find the selling cost.

$$\text{Selling Cost} = \text{Payroll Cost} \div \text{Net Sales}$$
$$= 4,100 \div 23,000$$
$$= 17.8\%$$

    b. Lowering the selling cost by 2% means: $17.8\% - 2\% = 15.8\%$.

$$\text{Selling Cost} = \text{Payroll Cost} \div \text{Net Sales}$$
$$15.8\% = 4,100 \div \text{Net Sales}$$

Multiplying both sides of the equation by net sales and dividing both sides by 15.8% yields:

$$\text{Net Sales} = 4,100 \div 15.8\%$$
$$= 25,949$$

To lower the selling cost by 2% will require net sales of $26,000.

Example 2:

A large toy store has net sales of $37,000 for June, and payroll cost of $7,500.

    a. Find the selling cost,

    b. Find reduction in the payroll cost needed to effect a 3% decrease in selling cost while keeping the same net sales.

Solution:

    a. Selling Cost = Payroll Cost ÷ Net Sales

$$= 7,500 \div 37,000$$
$$= 20.3\%$$

b. The new selling cost is to be $20.3\% - 3\% = 17.3\%$.

$$\text{Selling Cost} = \text{Payroll Cost} \div \text{Net Sales}$$
$$17.3\% = \text{Payroll Cost} \div 37{,}000$$

Multiplying both sides of the equation by 37,000 yields:

$$17.3\% \times 37{,}000 = \text{Payroll Cost}$$
$$\text{Payroll Cost} = \$6{,}401$$

The payroll cost needs to be reduced by about $1,100.

PRACTICE 20.3

1. A retailer has March net sales of $47,000. Her payroll cost is $8,100. Find:
   a. The selling cost,
   b. The net sales needed to effect a 3% decrease in selling cost while keeping the same payroll cost.

2. A department store has net sales of $247,000 for July and a payroll cost of $63,700.
   a. Find the selling cost,
   b. Find reduction in payroll cost needed to effect a 2.5% decrease in selling cost while keeping the same net sales.

CHAPTER TEST

1. Clara Trevor is paid $420 a week. Her sales last week were $3,970. Find her selling cost.

2. Carlos Ayala is the buyer for a men's wear department. His planned selling cost for the department for February is 12.5%. His planned net sales are $21,600. Find his wages.

Table 20–2 shows net sales for last year and this year as well as payroll cost for last year and this year.

3. By looking at Table 20–2, determine which selling cost definitely decreased from last year to this year.

4. Find the selling cost for jewelry last year.

5. Find the selling cost for jewelry this year.

6. Find the combined selling cost for the two departments last year.

7. Find the combined selling cost for the two departments this year.

8. Find the increase or decrease in selling cost from last year to this year.

9. A retailer has September net sales of $168,000. The payroll cost is $28,100. Find:
   a. The selling cost,
   b. The net sales needed to effect a 3.5% decrease in selling cost while keeping the same payroll cost. Round answer to the nearest hundred.

10. A department store has net sales of $415,000 for August and a payroll cost of $90,100.
   a. Find the selling cost,
   b. Find the payroll cost needed to effect a 2% decrease in selling cost while keeping the same net sales. Round answer to the nearest hundred.

TABLE 20–2

Payroll Cost

Department	Net Sales: Last Year	Net Sales: This Year	Payroll Cost: Last Year	Payroll Cost: This Year
Appliances	$54,400	$60,600	$11,700	$13,000
Jewelry	$102,000	$104,500	$17,500	$17,500

ANSWERS

20.1 1. 12.1%
2. $1,168.50
3. $1,750

20.2 1. Clothing
2. Sports
3. 11.9%
4. 12.2%
5. 15.2%
6. 15.1%
7. Decrease 0.1%

20.3 1. a. 17.2%, b. $57,042
2. a. 25.8%, b. $6149

CHAPTER TEST

1. 10.6%

2. $2,700

3. Jewelry

4. 17.2%

5. 16.7%

6. 18.7%

7. 18.5%

8. 0.2% decrease

9. a. 16.7%, b. 212,500

10. a. 21.7%, b. $81,800

Part IV   Record Keeping

21   Inventory Valuation

You have seen throughout this book that businesses have a choice in the way they assign a value to inventory that is purchased for sale. A retailer might buy sweaters for $20.00 each and then price them at $40.00 each. What value should the retailer assign to each sweater that is in inventory: the cost of $20.00 or the retail price of $40.00 each? In this chapter we will consider the advantages and disadvantages of each method, and we will see why the retail value is more commonly used by retailers.

After completing this chapter you will be able to:

- Understand and explain the differences between the cost and retail methods of valuing inventory.

- Explain the advantages and disadvantages of each method of valuing inventory.

- Convert from one method to the other.

- Complete purchase journal forms.

- Solve problems, especially as related to the retail method.

- Use an inventory worksheet markup, markup percent, gross sales, net sale, and other financial indicators.

21.1 COST METHOD AND RETAIL METHOD OF VALUING INVENTORY

Using the cost method, a retailer keeps records of merchandise according to the amounts paid for the goods. For some businesses this type of financial record keeping is most appropriate. A restaurant, for example, does not sell items in the same form that they are purchased. Rather, the food is transformed through the mixing of ingredients and cooking. So a restaurant owner could not place a resale or retail value on a pound of potatoes. Consequently, it makes sense to keep records at cost value. Clearly a restaurant is not a retail business in the usual sense.

Other less conventional retail businesses, which are likely to use the cost valuing method, are those that deal with expensive items such as cars, jewelry, and works of art. Items of this type are usually bought and sold in small quantities, and the prices are often negotiable. Consequently, the dealer will want to keep records in cost dollars.

The main advantage of the cost method is that it requires less direct record keeping. The main disadvantage is that many financial forms cannot be completed and profits cannot be adequately measured until a physical inventory is taken. The reason for this is that goods, even those as simple as bars of soap or boxes of cereal, may have been purchased at different cost prices although they have the same retail price.

Most retail businesses maintain inventory dollar records based on retail value. A department store, small business, or chain of food stores values inventory at retail prices. This means the business keeps records of both the cost and the retail dollar amount for inventory. The cost records are needed to maintain records of bills paid and to be paid. The retail value is kept for a variety of other reasons.

The advantages of the retail method are:

1. The value of the inventory can be quickly established without resorting to a physical inventory.

2. A physical inventory can be taken more efficiently since retail prices are maintained for all items.

3. Markdowns and their effect on gross margin are readily available. Recall that gross margin is a business's earnings after deducting the costs directly connected with the goods sold.

4. Financial statements can be prepared more easily and at any time.

We shall now review the conversion from cost to retail value of goods. The method of valuing inventory does not affect the method of determining markup. We shall continue to base markup on the selling price. Therefore, we have the following equations:

1. Markup Percent (MU%) × Selling Price = Markup Amount

2. Cost + Markup Amount = Selling Price = 100%

The markup is based on selling price and so selling price is 100%. Therefore the cost as a percent is 100% less markup percent. This amount is called the complement of the markup percent. We can write two other equations.

3. Cost = Cost Percent (complement of MU%) × Selling Price

4. Selling Price = Cost ÷ Cost Percent (Complement of MU%)

Example 1:

A shipment of shoes is purchased for $4,000 and receives a markup of 42%. Find the selling price.

Solution:

We can find the selling price by first finding the complement of the markup percent and then using equation (4).

Markup percent = 100% − 42% = 58%

Selling price = Cost ÷ Cost percent (complement of MU%)
= 4,000 ÷ 58%
= 6,896.55

The selling price is $6,896.55.

Example 2:

Inventory in a food store has a retail value of $12,380. The cost was $8,500. Find:

1. The markup amount,

2. The markup percent.

Solution:

1. Markup amount is the difference between the retail value and the cost: 12,380 − 8,500 = 3,880.

2. Markup percent can be found using the equation:

$$\text{Markup Percent} = \text{Markup Amount} \div \text{Selling Price}$$
$$= 3,880 \div 12,380$$
$$= 31.3\%$$

PRACTICE 21.1

1. Explain the difference between the cost method and the retail method of valuing inventory.

2. Describe a business for which the cost method would be preferred.

A clothing store purchases goods for $5,400 and places them on sale for a total of $8,000.

3. Find the markup amount.

4. Find the markup percent.

A toy store has inventory with a total retail value of $16,700. A markup of 45% was placed on the goods.

5. Find the complement of 45%.

6. Find the cost price of the goods.

7. A gift store has merchandise with a cost price of $15,200. The markup is 44%. Find the selling price of the goods, rounded to the nearest dollar.

21.2 THE PURCHASES JOURNAL

A retail business must maintain careful records of items purchased. The way in which these records are kept may vary, but the purchases journal

TABLE 21–1

Purchases Journal

Date	Vendor	Inventory Number	Quantity	Cost	Retail	MU%	Discount %	Discount Amount
3/14	PN	38,765	24	96.20	168.77	43	1	0.96
3/25	RT	39,020	350	674.40	1,226.18	45	2	13.49
3/31	PN	39,178	186	1,812.66	3,266.65	44.5	1	18.13

is a standard method. The purchases journal is a chronological list of items bought for resale. The partial purchases journal in Table 21–1 shows some of the standard information kept in such a journal.

Note each column of the form and the information contained in it.

Date: The journal is chronological; dates will be in order.

Vendor: The name or initials of the seller or supplier.

Invoice Number: Taken from the invoice at the time of the order.

Quantity: The number of items purchased.

Cost: Total amount charged for that order.

Retail: Retail price for the goods in that order.

MU%: The percent markup.

Discount %: The discount percent depends on the terms.

Discount Amount: Found by multiplying the cost by the discount percent.

PRACTICE 21.2

Use your knowledge of cost, retail value, markup, and discount to solve the problems, based on the information given in Table 21–2.

1. Find the retail value of the goods purchased on April 5.

2. Find the discount amount for the goods purchased on April 5.

TABLE 21–2

Purchases Journal

Date	Vendor	Inventory Number	Quantity	Cost	Retail	MU%	Discount %	Discount Amount
4/5	RT	39,554	80	342.90		43	2	
4/15	RT	39,871	225	803.50	1,460.90			16.07
4/21	PN	40,215	144		1,221.62	44.5	1	

3. Find the markup percent for the goods purchased with invoice 39871.

4. Find the discount percent for the goods purchased with invoice 39871.

5. Find the cost of the goods purchased on April 21.

6. Find the discount amount for the goods purchased on April 21.

21.3 INVENTORY WORKSHEET

We have seen that the retail method of valuing inventory requires that a business keep records of both cost and retail values of items. With computers and universal product codes, this record keeping is now easier and quicker than it used to be.

The computer spreadsheet in Figure 21–1 shows cost of goods purchased, the retail value of goods, the markup, and the markup percent.

The explanation of the spreadsheet columns follows:

A. Title.

B. Inventory and related expenses at cost value.

C. Inventory and related expenses at retail value.

D. Markup as dollar values.

E. Markup as percents.

FIGURE 21–1

	A	B	C	D	E
		Cost	Retail	Markup	Markup %
1					
2	Opening inventory	54000	90000	36000	40
3	Gross purchases	97320	149300		
4	Returns	6520	10000		
5	Net purchases (3 - 4)	90800	139300	48500	34.8
6	Transfers-in	8630	13700		
7	Transfers-out	630	1000		
8	Net transfers-in (6 - 7)	8000	12700	4700	37
9	Transportation costs	920			
10	Additional markups		2000		
11	Total merchandise	153720	244000	90280	37
	(2 + 5 + 8 + 9 + 10)				
12	Gross sales		115000		
13	Returns		15000		
14	Net sales (12 - 13)		100000		
15	Net markdowns		5000		
16	Retail deductions (14 + 15)		105000		
17	Book retail inventory (11 - 17)		139000		
18					

The explanation of the spreadsheet rows follows:

1. *Titles.*

2. *Opening Inventory:* The value of inventory on hand at the start of the fiscal period, which may be a month, a quarter, or a year.

3. *Gross Purchases:* Purchases made during the fiscal period.

4. *Returns:* The value of merchandise returned to vendors.

5. *Net purchases:* The difference between gross purchases and returns.

6. *Transfers-in:* The value of stock received from other stores.

7. *Transfers-out:* The value of stock sent to other stores.

8. *Net transfers-in:* The difference between transfers-in and transfers-out.

9. *Transportation costs:* Delivery charges paid by the retailer.

10. *Additional markups:* Increases in retail prices.

11. *Total Merchandise:* The sum of all amounts associated with purchases. Based on cost, these include items located in cells A2, A5, A8, and A9. Some of these are subtotals. Based on retail value, these include items located in cells B2, B5, B8, and B10.

12. *Gross sales:* The total retail value of sales.

13. *Returns:* The value of merchandise that customers have returned to the store.

14. *Net sales:* Gross sales less returns.

15. *Net markdowns:* Reductions in selling price.

16. *Retail deductions:* Net sales plus net markdowns. Both sales and markdowns reduce the retail value of inventory, even though they are different.

17. *Book retail inventory:* The difference between retail total merchandise amount and the total reductions in retail inventory. This is the retail value of the inventory at the close of the fiscal period.

PRACTICE 21.3

Answer the following based on your knowledge of the inventory worksheet.

1. What is the meaning of opening inventory?

2. What is the meaning of net transfers-in?

3. What is the meaning of total merchandise?

Use the inventory worksheet in Figure 21–2 to answer the items that follow.

4. Find the markup for the opening inventory.

5. Find the markup percent for opening inventory.

FIGURE 21–2

	A	B	C	D	E
1		Cost	Retail	Markup	Markup %
2	Opening inventory	44000	80000		
3	Gross purchases	65400	123400		
4	Returns	3200	5000		
5	Net purchases (3 − 4)	62200	118400	56200	
6	Transfers-in	4500	8300		
7	Transfers-out	1400	1000		
8	Net transfers-in (6 − 7)	3100	7300	4200	57.5
9	Transportation costs	550			
10	Additional markups		2000		
11	Total merchandise (2 + 5 + 8 + 9 + 10)	109850	207700		
12	Gross sales		82000		
13	Returns		7000		
14	Net sales (12 − 13)		75000		
15	Net markdowns		4000		
16	Retail deductions				
17	Book retail inventory (11 − 16)				
18					

6. Find the markup percent for net purchases.

7. Find the markup for total merchandise.

8. Find the markup percent for total merchandise.

9. Find the retail deductions.

10. Find the book retail inventory.

CHAPTER TEST

1. Explain the difference between the cost method and the retail method of valuing inventory and state one advantage of each method.

A sports store purchases goods for $6,400.00 and places them on sale for a total of $9,000.00.

2. Find the markup amount.

3. Find the markup percent.

A toy store has inventory with a total retail value of $21,500. A markup of 44% is placed on the goods.

4. Find the complement of 44%.

5. Find the cost price of the goods.

Use your knowledge of cost, retail value, markup, and discount to solve the problems, based on the information given in Table 21–3.

6. Find the cost value of the goods purchased on August 10.

7. Find the discount amount for the goods purchased on August 10.

8. Find the markup percent for the goods purchased with invoice 17652.

9. Find the discount amount for the goods purchased with invoice 17652.

10. Find the retail value of the goods purchased on August 29.

11. Find the discount percent for the goods purchased on August 29.

TABLE 21–3

Purchases Journal

Date	Vendor	Inventory Number	Quantity	Cost	Retail	MU%	Discount %	Discount Amount
8/10	JJ	17,630	24		198.00	45	1	
8/21	JJ	17,652	72	1,200	2,400		1	
8/29	TV	17,661	800	15,200		44		228

21.1
1. The cost method values inventory based on the amount paid for it; the retail method bases the value on the selling price.
2. An antique store which has many one-of-a-kind items and in which prices are often negotiated.
3. $2,600
4. 32.5%
5. 55%
6. $9,185
7. $27,143

21.2
1. $538.35
2. $6.86
3. 45%
4. 2%
5. $678
6. $6.80

21.3
1. Value of inventory at the start of a fiscal period.
2. Value of stock received from other stores.
3. The sum of all amounts directly related to purchases.
4. $36,000
5. 45%
6. 47.5%
7. $97,850
8. 47.1%
9. $79,000
10. $128,700

CHAPTER TEST

1. The cost method maintains records of inventory value based on the amounts paid for them. This method has the advantage of keeping track of the actual amounts. The retail method maintains records based on retail prices. This method has the advantage of being consistent with prices that are the basis for other financial records and reports.

2. $2,600

3. 28.9%

4. 56%

5. $12,040

6. $108.90

7. $1.09
8. 50%
9. $12
10. $27,143
11. 1.5%

22 Comparing Departments

The managers of department stores continually look for ways to increase sales and profits. They compare one department with another to see if each is contributing as much as can be expected to the overall business of the store. In this chapter we consider some of the methods used in these comparisons.

After completing this chapter you will be able to:

- Explain and calculate gross margin and profit dollars per square foot.
- Calculate gross margin percent.
- Calculate profit percent.
- Solve problems related to a department's contribution to a business.

22.1 SQUARE FEET

You have seen in previous chapters that the space a department occupies can be measured in square feet. This is a useful figure for several reasons.

First, the store is rented so the amount that is paid can be prorated by department. That is, a part of the rental amount can be assigned to each department. Second, space is valuable. Whatever space is occupied by one department cannot be used by another. So if a department is not getting the most from its space, the manager might decide to decrease the size of the department and increase the space of another department.

Example:

The Major Appliances department has net sales of $500,000 and takes 1,800 square feet. Find the net sales per square foot for the department.

Solution:

The amount per square foot can be found by dividing:

$$\text{Total sales} \div \text{Square feet} = \text{Sales per square foot}$$
$$500,000 \div 1,800 = 278$$

The sales per square foot equal $278.

PRACTICE 22.1

Find the sales per square foot for each department correct to the nearest dollar.

Department	Net Sales	Square Feet
1. Cosmetics	$875,000	3,900
2. Men's sportswear	350,000	1,800
3. Junior sportswear	530,000	2,800
4. Domestics	315,000	2,200
5. Housewares	400,000	3,800
6. Boy's Wear	300,000	3,300

22.2 COMPARING GROSS MARGIN

Sales and sales per square foot are not the only measures of a department's contribution to a company. A department might have high sales and high sales per square foot, but if the markup on its products is low, then the gross margin for the department might be lower than that of other departments. Recall that gross margin is the amount of money that is left to a business or department after the total cost of goods sold has been subtracted. The cost of goods sold includes the amount paid for the product and other costs directly associated with the purchases, such as delivery charges and alterations.

The gross margin percent for a department can be calculated by dividing the gross margin by net sales. In the previous section of this chapter you saw that the Major Appliances department had the highest net sales per square foot. But you will see from what follows that a manager would have other considerations when comparing departments.

Example 1:

The gross margin for Major Appliances is $120,000. Net sales are $500,000. Find the gross margin percent.

Solution:

To find the gross margin percent, we divide.

Gross margin dollars ÷ Net sales dollars = Gross margin percent
120,000 ÷ 500,000 = 0.24 = 24%

The gross margin percent is 24%.

Example 2:

Find the gross margin per square foot for Major Appliances. Recall that the Major Appliances department occupies 1,800 square feet.

Gross margin dollars ÷ square feet = Gross margin per square foot
120,000 ÷ 1,800 = $67.00

PRACTICE 22.2

Find the gross margin per square foot correct to the nearest dollar.

Department	Gross Margin	Square Feet	Gross Margin per Square Feet
1. Cosmetics	$350,000	3,900	
2. Men's Sportswear	150,500	1,800	
3. Junior Sportswear	243,800	2,800	
4. Domestics	119,700	2,200	
5. Housewares	164,000	3,800	
6. Boys' Wear	129,000	3,300	

Find the gross margin percent for each.

Department	Net Sales	Gross Margin	Gross Margin Percent
7. Cosmetics	$875,000	$350,000	
8. Men's Sportswear	350,000	150,500	
9. Junior Sportswear	530,000	243,800	
10. Domestics	315,000	119,700	
11. Housewares	400,000	164,000	
12. Boys' Wear	300,000	129,000	

22.3 COMPARING OPERATING PROFITS

There is still another measure that can be used to compare departments. This measure is operating profit. One department might have a better gross margin than another but because it requires a larger number of salespersons, it might show a lower profit.

Operating profit is the amount left after all expenses have been deducted from the net sales amount. Operating profit percent is found by dividing net profit by net sales.

Example 1:

The Major Appliances department had an operating profit of $45,000. Recall that net sales were $500,000. Find the operating profit percent.

Solution:

$$\text{Operating Profit} \div \text{Net Sales} = \text{Operating Profit Percent}$$
$$45{,}000 \div 500{,}000 = 0.09 = 9\%$$

The operating profit is 9%.

Example 2:

The operating profit for the Cosmetics department was 16% of net sales. Net sales amounted to $875,000. Find the dollar value of the operating profit.

Solution:

$$\text{Net Sales} \times \text{Operating Profit \%} = \text{Operating Profit}$$
$$875{,}000 \times 16\% = 140{,}000$$

The operating profit for the Cosmetics department is $140,000.

PRACTICE 22.3

Find the operating profit percent for each.

	Net Sales	Operating Profit	Operating Profit %
1. Men's Sportswear	350,000	66,500	
2. Junior Sportswear	530,000	137,800	

Find the operating profit for each.

	Net Sales	Operating Profit %	Operating Profit
3. Domestics	315,000	13%	
4. Housewares	400,000	10%	
5. Boys' Wear	300,000	17%	

Find the operating profit per square foot correct to the nearest cent.

	Operating Profit	Square Feet	Operating Profit per Square Feet
6. Men's Sportswear	66,500	10,500	
7. Junior Sportswear	137,000	28,800	

CHAPTER TEST

For each department find the sales per square foot correct to the near-est cent.

Department	Net Sales	Square Feet
1. Toys	$150,000	1,400
2. Infants' Wear	200,000	2,300

Find the gross margin percent for each.

Department	Net Sales	Gross Margin	GM Percent
3. Toys	$150,000	$67,500	
4. Infants' Wear	200,000	75,000	

Find the operating profit for each.

Department	Net Sales	Operating Profit %	Operating Profit
5. Toys	$150,000	23%	
6. Infants' Wear	200,000	18%	

ANSWERS

22.1	1.	$224
	2.	$194
	3.	$189
	4.	$143
	5.	$105
	6.	$91

22.2	1.	$90
	2.	$84
	3.	$87
	4.	$54
	5.	$43
	6.	$39
	7.	40%
	8.	43%
	9.	46%
	10.	38%
	11.	41%
	12.	43%

22.3	1.	19%
	2.	26%
	3.	$40,950
	4.	$40,000
	5.	$51,000
	6.	$6.33
	7.	$4.76

CHAPTER TEST

1. $107.14

2. $86.96

3. 45%

4. 37.5%

5. $34,500

6. $36,000

23   The Income Statement

The owners of retail stores, businesses, and companies generally know whether they are successful or not based on sales volume and the cash generated by sales. But they also need more accurate and detailed information about the performance of the business. Financial statements fill this need.

After completing this chapter you will be able to:

- Explain and interpret the information on an income statement.

- Complete an income statement.

- Explain and interpret the information on a balance sheet.

- Complete a balance sheet.

23.1 GROSS MARGIN AND NET INCOME

The *income statement* is a financial document that shows sales and expenses for a particular period of time. The five major categories of the income statement are as follows:

Net Sales: The dollar amount of sales less returns.

Cost of Goods Sold (C.O.G.S.):   The amount paid for the items sold. This also includes amounts directly related to the acquisition of the products, such as delivery charges and alteration fees.

Gross Margin (also called Gross Profit):   The amount remaining after C.O.G.S. has been subtracted from net sales.

Operating Expenses: Additional expenses needed to operate a business, such as wages for employees, rent, utilities expense, and supplies.

Net Income: The amount remaining after operating expenses have been subtracted from gross margin.

The Corner Clothier is a retail clothing store. Its sales and expenses for April are as follows:

Net Sales	$18,400
C.O.G.S.	9,900
Gross Margin	8,500
Operating Expenses	6,300
Net Income	2,200

To find the gross margin percent you divide.

$$\text{Gross Margin} \div \text{Net Sales} = \text{Gross Margin \%}$$
$$8{,}500 \div 18{,}400 \quad = 0.46$$
$$= 46\%$$

The net income percent can be found in a similar way.

$$\text{Net Income} \div \text{Net Sales} = \text{Net Income \%}$$
$$2{,}200 \div 18{,}400 \quad = 0.12$$
$$= 12\%$$

PRACTICE 23.1

The True-Step Shoe Store's sales for the fourth quarter (last three months) are as follows:

Net Sales	$102,500
C.O.G.S.	59,200
Gross Margin	
Operating Expenses	27,100
Net Income	

1. Find the gross margin.

2. Find the gross margin percent correct to the nearest tenth.

3. Find the net income.

4. Find the net income percent correct to the nearest tenth.

The Kiddie Carousel, a children's clothing store, had annual net sales of $176,500; C.O.G.S. was $94,300 and operating expenses were $53,200.

5. Find the gross margin.

6. Find the gross margin percent.

7. Find the net income.

8. Find the net income percent.

23.2 THE INCOME STATEMENT

The income statement contains several subcategories of the five main categories that you worked with in the previous section. For example, the amount of returns must be subtracted from total sales in order to find net sales. Purchases during the month must be added to opening inventory and there are a variety of expenses to be considered under operating expenses.

The form in Figure 23–1 is a simplified income statement. Transfers-in and out, reductions, and markdowns are all included in the category Inventory E.O.M. Note that the five main categories provide the basic structure for the statement.

PRACTICE 23.2

Use the income statement in Figure 23–1 to answer the following.

1. Find the gross margin as a percent of net sales.

2. Find the total operating expense as a percent of net sales.

3. Find the net income as a percent of net sales.

Globe Department Store
Income Statement
Month Ending March 31

Sales	221,400	
Less Returns	8,700	
Net Sales..		212,700
C.O.G.S.		
Inventory, B.O.M.	356,100	
Purchases..	65,800	
Total Inventory	421,900	
Less Inventory E.O.M..	305,200	
Cost of Goods Sold		116,700
Gross Margin		96,000
Operating Expenses		
Salaries	56,400	
Rent...	4,200	
Utilities/Supplies	7,300	
Miscellaneous Expense......................................	8,700	
Total Operating Expense		76,600
Net Income		19,400

FIGURE 23–1

Simple income
statement.

CHAPTER TEST

Complete the income statement using Figure 23–2 by finding the missing amounts.

7. Find C.O.G.S. as a percent of net sales.

8. Find operating expenses as a percent of net sales.

9. Find net income as a percent of net sales.

10. What is the income statement?

Globe Department Store
Income Statement
Month Ending April 30

Sales..	256,400	
Less Returns...	10,700	
Net Sales		1. _____
C.O.G.S.		
Inventory, B.O.M.....................................	305,200	
Purchases...	65,200	
Total Inventory		2. _____
Less Inventory E.O.M.	245,200	
Cost of Goods Sold.............................		3. _____
Gross Margin		4. _____
Operating Expenses		
Salaries...	57,300	
Rent	4,900	
Utilities/Supplies....................................	6,700	
Miscellaneous Expense	7,200	
Total Operating Expense...................		5. _____
Net Income		6. _____

FIGURE 23–2

Income statement.

ANSWERS

23.1 1. $43,300
2. 42.2%
3. $16,200
4. 15.8%
5. $82,200
6. 46.6%
7. $29,000
8. 16.4%

23.2 1. 45.1%
2. 36%
3. 9.1%

CHAPTER TEST

1. $245,700

2. $370,400

3. $125,200

4. $120,500

5. $76,100

6. $44,400

7. 51%

8. 31%

9. 18.1%

10. A report that states the important finances of a business during a given time period.

Appendix

Math Review

■ MR-1 PLACE VALUE

Figure A–1 shows place value from millions to hundredths. As a dollar amount, the number is $4,781,256.39 and we read it: Four million, seven hundred eighty-one thousand, two hundred fifty-six dollars and thirty-nine cents. Notice that we say "and" at the decimal point.

The digits 0 to 9 have different meanings depending on where they appear in a number. For example, the 8 in the above number means $80,000. The whole number is equal to the sum of the amounts for each place in the number.

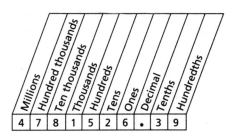

FIGURE A–1

Example:

Identify the place value of the 5 and the amount of money represented by the 5 in the number $76,523.01.

Solution:

The place value chart shows that the 5 is in the hundreds place. The 5 stands for $500.00.

PRACTICE MR-1

Identify the place value of the 6 and the amount of money represented by the 6 in each number.

1. $6,000.00   2. $560.89
3. $7,682,031   4. $76.23
5. $402.56   6. $6,800,325

MR-2 ROUNDING

To round a number, we first consider the place to which we will round:

1. Consider the digit in the rounding place, that is, the units place.

2. Look at the digit to the right of the number in the rounding place.

3. (a) If the digit to the right of the rounding place is 5 or greater, increase the digit in the rounding place by 1 and affix 0s as needed.

   (b) If the digit to the right of the rounding place is less than 5, leave the digit in the rounding place unchanged and affix 0s as needed.

Example:

Round $56.54 to the nearest dollar.

Solution:

The number in the rounding place is 6.
The number to the right of the 6 is 5.
Five is "5 or greater."
Round up to $57.

Practice MR-2

Round each number to the nearest dollar.

1. $52.45   2. $701.60
3. $70.99   4. $4,599.50

Round each to the nearest hundred dollars.

5. $57,830   6. $780,555
7. $1,239,990   8. $4,310.00

MR-3 ADDING DECIMALS

When adding amounts of money or other decimal numbers, it is important to align the decimal points. This allows you to add according to place value, that is, to add cents to cents, dollars to dollars, and so on.

To add $506.78, $7.00, $3,710.03, $99.98 without a calculator, first rewrite the numbers with decimal points aligned:

$ 506.78	Add as you would add whole numbers.
7.00	Begin with the right-hand column.
3,710.03	Carry as needed.
99.98	
$4,323.79	Align the decimal point in the answer.

SUBTRACTING DECIMALS

Subtraction of decimals follows the same rules as the subtraction of whole numbers. Subtraction can be checked by adding the number subtracted to the answer.

	Check:
$1,005.07	$ 577.99
− 577.99	+427.08
427.08	$1,005.77

PRACTICE MR-3

Rewrite and add or subtract as indicated:

1. $567.89 + $312.67
2. $1,230.78 − $523.99
3. $45.68 + $328.15 + $6.77
4. $700.00 − $15.99
5. $1,345.08 − $458.33
6. $805.00 + 77.99

MR-4 CONVERTING BETWEEN PERCENTS AND DECIMALS

We now review the meaning of percent and how to solve percent problems using the calculator.

Percent means parts out of 100. There are 100 cents in $1.00 so 17 percent means 17 cents. 17% of $1.00 is $0.17.

Decimals are read and understood as tenths, hundredths, and thousandths. So you can convert between decimals and percents. To convert from decimals to percents, move the decimal point two places to the right and add a percent sign.

For example, 0.3 is equal to 0.30, and this can be converted to 30%.

To convert 0.455 to a percent, move the decimal point two places: 0.455 = 45.5%.

To convert 1.50 to a percent, move the decimal point two places to the right: 1.50 = 150%.

Percents can be converted to decimals by taking away the percent sign and moving the decimal point two places to the left. If there is no decimal point, insert one after the number, before the percent sign.

For example, 60% = 0.60 or 0.6.

To convert 3% to a decimal, write 0.03. This is read three-hundredths.

PRACTICE MR-4

Convert each of the following decimals to a percent.

1. 0.90   2. 0.02
3. 0.635   4. 3.40
5. 0.025   6. 1.1

Convert each percent to a decimal.

7. 10%   8. 5%
9. 12.5%   10. 125%
11. 50%   12. 500%

MR-5 FINDING THE PERCENT OF A NUMBER

To find the percent of a number, convert the percent to a decimal and then multiply by the number.

For example, to find 25% of $45.00, first convert 25% to a decimal, then multiply the decimal by $45.00.

$$25\% = 0.25$$
$$0.25 \times 45 = 11.25$$

Therefore, 25% of $45.00 equals $11.25.

Example:

Find 7.5% of $145.60.

Solution:

Change 7.5% to a decimal: 7.5% = 0.075
Enter $145.60 × 0.075 =
Read the answer: 10.92

Therefore, 7.5% of $145.60 is $10.92.

CALCULATOR REVIEW

Business calculators have a small switch called a decimal selector. This selector tells the calculator how to round an answer. When dealing with money you will usually want an answer to be in dollars and cents. For example, if you divide 176 by 7, you want an answer to be 25.14 not 25.14285714. To obtain the first answer you set the calculator decimal selector at 2.

PRACTICE MR-5

Set the decimal selector at 2.

25% of $4.50   Answer $1.13

1. 7% of $813.00

2. 5.5% of $78.65

3. 40% of $1035.80

4. 140% of $19.46

MR-6 THE PERCENT EQUATION

In most percent problems there are three numbers:

p: the *percent* itself, the number with the percent sign.

b: the *base*, the number for which you are finding percent.

a: the *amount*, the product of multiplying the base by the percent.

The triangle in Figure A–2 can help you remember the arithmetic used in percent. In equation form, we write, $a = pb$. In the triangle p and b are adjacent. This reminds us that we multiply them to find a. But a is over b. This reminds us that if we know a and b, we divide to find p. Similarly if we know a and p, we divide to find b.

Example:

$45.00 is what percent of $120.00? 45 is the amount; 120 is the base. To find the percent, p, we divide. Using the calculator: Enter 45. Press the division sign. Enter 120. Read: 0.3750. The answer is 37.5%.

FIGURE A–2

PRACTICE MR-6

Find each percent. Set the decimal selector at 4. Round answers to the nearest tenth.

1. $12.00 is what percent of $80.00? _____

2. $21.00 is what percent of $42.00? _____

3. $4.00 is what percent of $12.00? _____

4. $45.00 is what percent of $60.00? _____

5. $35.00 is what percent of $60.00? _____

MR-7 FINDING THE BASE

The percent equation can be used to find the base when the percent and amount are known.

Example:

$15.00 is 30% of a certain number. What is the number?

Solution:

First write the percent equation: $a = p \times b$
The number is the amount, so: $15 = 30\% \times b$
Therefore, $15 = 0.3 \times b$
Divide both sides by 0.3: $15 \div 0.3 = b$
$50 = b$

The base is 50. Therefore, $15 = 30\% \times 50$. This checks.

PRACTICE MR-7

1. 5 is 20% of what number?

2. $34.00 is 200% of what number?

3. $4.40 is 2.5% of what number?

4. $247.50 is 55% of what number?

5. $667.50 is 75% of what number?

ANSWERS

MR-1
1. thousands, $6,000
2. tens, $60
3. hundred thousands, $600,000
4. ones, $6
5. hundredths, $0.06
6. millions, $6,000,000

MR-2
1. $52
2. $702
3. $71
4. $4,600
5. $57,800
6. $780,600
7. $1,240,000
8. $4,300

MR-3
1. $880.56
2. $706.79
3. $380.60
4. $684.01
5. $886.75
6. $882.99

MR-4
1. 90%
2. 2%
3. 63.5%
4. 340%
5. 2.5%
6. 110%
7. 0.1
8. 0.05
9. 0.125
10. 1.25
11. 0.5
12. 5

MR-5
1. $56.91
2. $4.32
3. $414.32
4. $27.24

MR-6
1. 15%
2. 50%
3. 33.3%
4. 75%
5. 58.3%

MR-7
1. $25
2. $17
3. $176
4. $450
5. $890

Index

297